Word Processing:
A SYSTEMS APPROACH TO THE OFFICE

Helen M. McCabe
LaGuardia Community College of the City University of
New York

Estelle L. Popham
Professor Emeritus, Hunter College of the City University
of New York

Word Processing

A SYSTEMS APPROACH TO THE OFFICE

HARCOURT BRACE JOVANOVICH, INC.
New York   Chicago   San Francisco   Atlanta

© 1977 by Harcourt Brace Jovanovich, Inc.

All rights reserved. No part of this publication may be
reproduced or transmitted in any form or by any means,
electronic or mechanical, including photocopy, recording,
or any information storage and retrieval system, without
permission in writing from the publisher.

ISBN: 0-15-596666-9

Library of Congress Catalog Card Number: 77-72103

Printed in the United States of America

Preface

This book is designed to introduce you to the changing office—the world of word processing, a relatively new and for many a mysterious world. We trust that *Word Processing: A Systems Approach to the Office* will remove some of the mystery.

What exactly is "word processing"? Following are definitions given by specialists in the field.

> "A managed system of people, procedures, and equipment for the handling of business communications."

> "The handling of the wordflow in an office in the most efficient and economical way possible."

> "The professional application of management science and technology to accomplish verbal communication with maximum productivity."

> "A program to improve the efficiency of business communications. The combination of people, procedures, and equipment in the proper system designed to meet the needs of an organization."

These definitions all emphasize the fact that the tasks of dictating, revising, typing, copying, and duplicating are being transformed into an integrated system of controlled, automated procedures.

Word processing came into existence in the mid-1960s with the introduction of the automatic electric typewriter—an electronic marvel that types out error-free work at speeds many times that of the typical typist. But word processing is more than equipment. It is a systems approach to office management that directly affects the secretary—in fact, the whole office.

Traditionally, an executive dictated to a personal secretary, who took shorthand notes and then transcribed them into typewritten copy. The secretary did many other things, however. She (and it was usually a she) was a "take charge" person, an invaluable assistant, who, in addition to her regular work, kept track of personal accounts for income tax purposes, maintained personal files, and brewed coffee—to name but a few tasks.

The need for such secretaries continues to exist, as witness the help-wanted section of any metropolitan newspaper. But because of technological developments, ways of producing written communications are changing. Organizations large and small, snowed under by vast amounts of paperwork, are finding it advisable to purchase new automatic equipment and to restructure their offices so that words can be processed in centers devoted exclusively to that function. The result is a systems approach to the office that divides secretarial work into specialized tasks and roles: (1) the correspondence secretary who works in a word processing center and transcribes on modern equipment the work generated by "principals," or executives; (2) the administrative support secretary who handles the work of several executives—for example, answering the telephone, greeting callers, arranging meetings, and working out itineraries.

Just as electronic data processing revolutionized manufacturing operations and accounting, word processing is bringing about revolutionary changes in the contemporary office structure. In effect, EDP is to quantitative data or numbers what WP is to qualitative data or words. It therefore behooves secretarial science students, as well as anyone planning a career in the business management field, to understand the word processing concept and how it relates to them. We hope this book will further that understanding.

Helen M. McCabe
Estelle L. Popham

Contents

	PREFACE	v
chapter 1	INTRODUCTION TO WORD PROCESSING AND WORD PROCESSING SYSTEMS	1
	New Office Job Titles and Responsibilities	2
	Historical Development of Secretarial/Clerical Work	6
	Changing Secretarial/Clerical Positions	7
	Need for the Office to Increase Output and Reduce Costs	8
	The Human Element in Word Processing	9
	Suggested Readings	10
chapter 2	THE DEVELOPMENT OF WORD PROCESSING EQUIPMENT	11
	Automatic Typewriters and Modern Word Processing	11
	Communicating Typewriters	17
	Second-Generation CRT or Microcomputer Word Processing Systems	18
	Importance of Dictation Equipment in Word Processing	22
	Centralized Dictation Equipment—Discrete Media	23
	Centralized Dictation Equipment—Endless Loop	26
	Types of Telephone Systems Used with Centralized Dictation	28
	Suggested Readings	30
chapter 3	WORD PROCESSING SYSTEMS—THEORY AND DEVELOPMENT	31
	A Systems Approach to Office Paperwork	31
	Word Processing and Word Processing Systems Defined	32
	Traditional Secretarial Positions	34
	The Nature of Secretarial Work	36

	Secretarial Utilization and Increasing Office Costs	37
	Traditional Methods of Dictation and Transcription	38
	Cost of Operation in the Word Processing Secretarial Mode	39
	Traditional Work Habits Affected by Word Processing Systems	40
	Administrative Support Function in Word Processing Systems	40
	The Administrative Zone—A Comprehensive Word Processing System	43
	Flexibility of Word Processing Systems	45
	Suggested Reading	46

chapter 4 WORD PROCESSING POSITIONS — 49

	Characteristics of a Word Processing Secretary	49
	Characteristics of an Administrative Secretary	50
	Position Descriptions	51
	Word Processing Job Titles	56
	Suggested Readings	57

chapter 5 HUMAN ASPECTS OF WORD PROCESSING TECHNOLOGY — 59

	The Challenge of the 1970s	59
	Automation and the Rationalization of Work	62
	Data Processing and the Division of Labor	63
	Word Processing and the Division of Labor	65
	The Administrative Support Side of Secretarial Work	65
	Career Paths for Administrative Secretaries	67
	The Word Processing Side of Secretarial Work	68
	The Mechanization of Office Work	69
	Employee Morale in Word Processing Centers	70
	People-Oriented Word Processing	74
	The Challenge of Automation Technology	76
	Suggested Readings	77

chapter 6 WORD PROCESSING CASE STUDIES — 79

	Case Study: Crown Center Hotel	80
	Case Study: Illinois National Bank of Springfield	82
	Case Study: State National Bank of Connecticut	83
	Case Study: Mountainside Hospital	84

	Case Study: Del Monte Corporation	85
	Case Study: Natural Resources Group of W. R. Grace & Company	87
	Case Study: Teachers Insurance and Annuity Association and College Retirement Equities Fund	88
	Case Study: CH2M Hill	90
	Case Study: Chevron Oil Company Geophysical Division	92
	Case Study: Congressional Research Service of the Library of Congress	94
	Case Study: Bergman & Barth	96
	Case Study: Houston Lighting & Power Company	98
	Suggested Readings	100

chapter 7 COMPUTER WORD PROCESSING   101

Historical Development of Computers	102
Development of Electronic Computers	103
First Generation of Commercial Computers	104
Second Generation of Computers	104
Third Generation of Computers	106
Use of Minicomputers	107
Computer Word Processing	108
Time Share Computing—Word Processing and Data Processing	109
Minicomputer Word Processing Systems	110
Manufacturers of Minicomputer Word Processing Systems	111
Microcomputers and the Second Computer Revolution	115
Microcomputer Word Processing Systems	116
Suggested Readings	116

chapter 8 WORD PROCESSING AND MANAGEMENT INFORMATION SYSTEMS   119

Telecommunications	121
Records Management	133
Executive Control and Organizational Structures	142
Suggested Readings	146

chapter 9 THE AUTOMATED PAPERLESS OFFICE OF THE FUTURE   147

Office Workers of the 1990s	148
Office Workers and Computers	149

Future Office Equipment 151
Future Office Procedures 153
Forces Affecting Organizational Structures 156
Two-Way Communication Between Management and
 Employees 157
Expanding Employment in Human Services 158
Future Office Management Systems 159
Suggested Readings 159

APPENDIX A   WORD PROCESSING PUBLICATIONS 161

APPENDIX B   SUPPLIERS OF WORD PROCESSING
 EQUIPMENT 163

GLOSSARY OF TERMS 165

INDEX 175

Word Processing:
A SYSTEMS APPROACH TO THE OFFICE

Chapter 1

INTRODUCTION TO WORD PROCESSING AND WORD PROCESSING SYSTEMS

Words have been processed ever since people began to write, but modern word processing began with the invention of the automatic electric typewriter. At the touch of a button, this marvelous machine is capable of typing out error-free documents at a speed three or more times that of a superior human typist. When combined with dictating machines, the automatic typewriter makes possible a systems approach to the processing of words. The introduction of this unique office machine has triggered a re-evaluation of the way in which business offices are organized. Traditional work patterns of white-collar workers, from top managers down to office clerks, are being systematically analyzed. New approaches to office paperwork are being instituted in order to take advantage of the automatic electric typewriter and modern word processing.

More and more offices appear to be making the transition to modern word processing and word processing systems. Broadly defined, word processing is the automatic production of typed documents or the automation of secretarial work.[1] The systems approach deals with office procedures, personnel, and equipment as an organized whole, rather than with each part separately. The routine tasks of dictating, typing, correcting, revising, copying, and duplicating correspondence and reports are being reorganized into a unified system of controlled, automated office procedures. Sophisticated machines combined with the systems approach of modern business management are in the process of transforming the inefficiently operated front office into a high-production, cost-efficient work environment, much as the computer and electronic data processing transformed back-of-the-house operations. Word processing in the office and electronic data processing in the factory share a similar goal—increased output and reduced costs.

In the 1960s, the use of computers and electronic data processing brought cost-saving automation to the factory and the accounting office in the processing of numbers. Before computers, numbers were processed by hand or by machines that required many time-consuming steps to make calculations. **Electronic data processing, however, employs electronic computers in recording, coding, sorting, calculating, summarizing, storing, and communicating business data.** These data include accounting, payroll, personnel, inventory, and production figures. Computers used in industry provide the speed and accuracy essential for production control, record maintenance, and efficient business management. If a business is to remain competitive, up-to-date and accurate information is needed for responsible management decisions. What electronic data processing is to numbers, word processing is to words.

The use of word processing equipment and modern work methods promises to bring under control the ever-increasing flood of paperwork and the rising costs of the office. Experts in the field of business administration and management are agreed in general that total office systems are coming. Word processing will provide the springboard from which executive and administrative offices will become automated. Within large and small corporations, organizations, institutions, and government agencies, word processing is responsible already for new, more efficient ways of organizing and completing office tasks.

NEW OFFICE JOB TITLES AND RESPONSIBILITIES

Help-wanted ads reflect some of the changes brought about by the word processing concept. An international trading company seeks a director of administrative services with knowledge of word processing in

---

[1] *Dartnell's Glossary of Word Processing Terms* (Chicago, 1975), p. 47.

> **Office Administrator**
> **Law Firm**
>
> Our client, a growth-oriented law firm is seeking to employ an Office Administrator to be *responsible for the performance and supervision of automated systems including: bookkeeping, billing, financial management, word processing, personnel management, purchasing, space planning,* etc. This individual should have a *working knowledge of EDP* along with *previous law office experience.*
>
> All responses kept in strictest confidence. Please send resume and earnings record to:
>
> **John J. Evans & Co. Inc.**
> Consultants to the Legal Profession
> **Central Towers Bldg.**
> **Philadelphia, Pa. 19103**
> An Equal Opportunity Employer M/F

addition to knowledge of communications and ability to plan work space and office layout.

A New York City-based firm seeks a word processing administrator with a thorough knowledge of typing operations, ability to analyze equipment, and appreciation of the word processing concept. Responsibilities include the most efficient use of an advanced word processing system, both manual and automatic, and the selection of the best qualified employees and the most efficient office methods, equipment, and layout for typing services.

An opening in a Wall Street firm for an office administrator requires someone who will assume responsibility for automated systems which include both word processing (WP) and electronic data processing (EDP).

Listings for brand-new clerical/secretarial positions are appearing in the help-wanted ads. In addition to the position of secretary, advertisements are also found for dictaphone secretary, mag card secretary, correspon-

DIRECTOR OF ADMINISTRATIVE SERVICES

for large international trading company located in Manhattan's Wall Street area. *Knowledge of communications, word processing,* and *facilities planning desired.*

Salary range: $15,000 to $20,000.

ADMIN ASST/SECRETARY
If you are one of the most organized admin asst secretaries in the NY area and are people-oriented, you will be interested in this challenging position.
YOU WILL...
...juggle many priorities at once (your own projects)
...create & admin systems & controls
...respond to varied communications and service requests from a national sales force.
...administer your own small clerical and bookkeeping staff.
...and most important of all, directly support our energetic President of this exciting growth company.
Send resume and salary requirements to X3849 GLOBE.

DICTAPHONE $160   FEE PAID
TRAIN MAG CARD
Top notch ad agency has multiple openings in their word processing center for skilled dictaphone typist w/60WPM typing to train on the Mag Card I. Excellent bfts & midtown loc. Call Joseph Wendling at 762-6381/Danforth Agency, 29 Somer St. Room 112.
SUNDAY CALLS INVITED

DICTAPHONE TYPIST
To work in word processing center. Should have at least 2 yrs previous exp. Excell salary, benefits and working conditions.
APPLY IN PERSON
Personnel Dept   8th Floor
UNITED MANUFACTURERS
2562 Pearl St.
Hartford, Connecticut 06107
An Equal Opportunity Employer

DICTAPHONE-MAG CARD II
Midtown real estate firm seeks individual with experience. Good knowledge of sentence structure, grammar, punctuation & spelling.
Hanlin Agency, 925 Madison Ave. (Rm. 706) 682-3415

TYPIST $OPEN   FEE PAID
TRAIN VYDEC
Fortune 500 firm seeks qualified VYDEC operators or persons with any word processing exp to assume diversified responsibilities. This is not a pool situation, so candidates should possess good phone voice & appearance. Beaut surroundings & exclnt mdtn loc. Definite advancement oppty. Call MARJE LEE at 764-6984.
Stevens Agency, 570 5th Ave/47th St.
SUNDAY CALLS INVITED

Word Process Op f/p $200 +
Top law firm seeks indiv exp in any of the following word processing machines: Xerox, Sperry Remington, Wang or Tydata.
Apply in person to:
Day, Berry & Lynch
345 North Main St.
Mon.-Fri., 9:00 AM—3:00 PM

WORD PROCESSING SUPV. $13K
Growing Engrg Co seeks talented individual to help set up dept.
Contact Ms Ellen Holliday for appointment
(617) 277-3566

---

dence secretary, word processing secretary, and administrative secretary. The titles indicate the specialized nature of each position. Frequently, the word "secretary" is omitted altogether and the position is listed under the brand name of the automatic typewriter. Mag card,

ADMINISTRATOR
Word Processing

Where can you best display your keen ability for totally efficient equipment and manpower utilization?

Our client has an excellent opportunity for you if you have at least 8 years experience that's given you a thorough *knowledge of typing operations, analysis of equipment, and a well-versed appreciation of the word processing concept.* Your background should show both supervisory and administrative ability.

Reporting to our client's *Manager of Administrative Services,* you'll have special responsibility for the most efficient use of their advanced *manual and automated word processing system,* as well as decisive responsibility for selecting the best qualified employees and most feasible office methods, equipment and layout suited to their typing services. Aptitude for productive, personal contact with department heads essential.

With this immediate opportunity to join a first-class administrative staff, our client offers an excellent salary and a full range of benefits. For consideration, forward your resume, including salary requirement, to:

Alice Fenwick Associates
Dept CJ, 755 Caldwell Avenue, Chicago, Ill. 60648
Our client is an equal opportunity employer M/F

Mag Card II, MT/ST, and MC/ST are all made by International Business Machines Corporation (IBM). Vydec, the Xerox ETS800, Redactron, Wang, Sperry Remington, and Tydata, also listed in the following ads, are different manufacturers of word processing machines.

These new kinds of secretarial positions are rapidly increasing. More and more corporate offices, government agencies, and law firms seek to control operating costs and increase productivity by investing in expensive word processing equipment. The new equipment in turn calls for new skills and job responsibilities on the part of clerical personnel, particularly secretaries.

In order to make clear the significance of these new kinds of secretarial positions, a brief look at the development of clerical work, from its origin in the nineteenth century to the present, will be helpful.

HISTORICAL DEVELOPMENT OF SECRETARIAL/CLERICAL WORK

The two basic skills required for the traditional position of secretary are shorthand and typing. The value of shorthand, however, was not fully recognized until the first commercial typewriter, the Remington No. 1, appeared in 1873. Before the Civil War, farming began to be replaced by factory labor as the major occupation of the American work force. Penmanship and bookkeeping were the most important skills required of office workers. After the Civil War, as business expanded during the reconstruction period and workers moved from the farms to the cities, the need for trained bookkeepers and stenographers steadily increased. There was also a large turnover in stenographic occupations, since the young male stenographers in business offices usually advanced to administrative positions.

For many years, students in the private business schools were mostly men and boys. Some schools actually offered free tuition to women to encourage them to study stenography. The middle class, at that time, considered teaching the only respectable work outside the home for women; working-class women were domestic servants or light factory workers. However, the idea of office work for women gradually became accepted, and shorthand and typing opened up new kinds of jobs for women of both classes.

Further improvements made the typewriter more efficient and more widely used in business. As a result, shorthand became increasingly important as an office skill. Typewriting and shorthand were not accepted overnight as a means of business communication, however. Public antagonism toward typewritten (as opposed to handwritten) letters was strong. For many years, conservative businessmen believed that typewritten letters were insulting. Customers resented them for being impersonal and for casting doubt on their ability to read longhand.

At the turn of the century, as large corporations rapidly replaced smaller enterprises, many new clerical and secretarial positions developed. Women were then actively recruited as office workers to fill jobs in industrial and financial institutions. By the early 1900s, the majority of students studying shorthand and typing in the private business schools were women. Whereas male stenographers had acted as stand-ins and possible successors to the boss, the promotional paths changed when women entered the labor market as secretaries. Secretarial jobs became low-paying, supplementary work, since employers considered women temporary workers who would leave their jobs once they married. Consequently, there was little or no chance for promotion to executive positions, a situation that is only somewhat improved today. The "temporary" work myth also persists to this day, although some 35 million women are in the work force, almost three fifths (58 percent) of them married and living with their husbands.

CHANGING SECRETARIAL/CLERICAL POSITIONS

Traditionally, the salary and status of a secretarial position depends on the salary and status of the executive for whom a secretary works, rather than on individual skills and abilities. Work tasks and responsibilities depend in large measure on the boss. Therefore, the traditional secretary is a generalist rather than a specialist. In order to achieve increased output and efficiency, greater specialization in work tasks and skills is needed. In organizations using word processing equipment, widespread changes in the generalized work tasks of secretaries are already under way. The new word processing position titles indicate the specialized nature of the tasks resulting from the reorganization of office personnel and procedures.

Word processing systems separate the traditional secretary's work into two categories: typing and nontyping duties. Typing then becomes the specialized function of the word processing secretary (sometimes called the correspondence secretary). The position requires a typing technician, a machine-oriented person who understands automated equipment and knows how to use its capabilities to best advantage. A word processing secretary needs good language skills, the ability to think through and solve problems, and the ability to handle many different types of documents and machines. The nontyping duties become the specialized function of the administrative secretary. This position requires a person with good human relations skills and the ability to provide essential administrative support to executives in handling their mail, telephones, files, and special projects as assigned.

A similar reorganization of clerical positions occurred in the 1960's when the positions of payroll clerk and inventory clerk were largely replaced by keypunch operator and digital-computer operator, positions introduced by electronic data processing. Additional changes in other clerical positions are anticipated. File clerk, mail clerk, telephone operator, and other positions are expected to take on a new look as a result of technological innovations brought about by new computers, duplicating, filing, and mailing equipment, and communication devices.

A survey by the Stanford Research Institute indicates that office costs formerly represented 20 to 30 percent of a company's total cost; today they represent 40 to 50 percent of the total.[2] According to IBM, the average salary for a secretary has increased 68 percent since 1965, and the cost of sending out a business letter has increased 40 percent.[3] Figures prepared by the Dartnell Corporation show that the average cost of a business letter was $4.17 in 1976, $3.79 in 1975, and $3.41 in 1974. Dartnell research shows that the difference in the annual costs reflects increases in both salary and materials. In 1976, secretaries' sala-

---

[2] "The Office of the Future," *Business Week* (June 30, 1975), p. 49.
[3] *Ibid.*

ries represented $1.17 of the total cost of a business letter, or an 11 percent increase in one year.[4]

Office workers' salaries, volume of information, and paperwork are growing at geometric rates; and the number of clerical job opportunities is fast expanding. Employment in clerical jobs is expected to rise to 19.7 million in 1985, up from 14.2 million in 1972.[5] To reduce costs, top management will have to adopt techniques used in electronic data processing and automated factory operations, where annual unit labor costs have steadily declined.

NEED FOR THE OFFICE TO INCREASE OUTPUT AND REDUCE COSTS

In a business the processing of words, whether by hand or by machine, is predominantly a clerical function. Clerical work is **labor-intensive; that is, labor costs comprise a major part of the total cost of running an office.** Although factory production costs were reduced significantly by eliminating inefficient operations through automation, little attempt was made until recently to automate the clerical or secretarial operations of the business office. With clerical salaries rising sharply, however, the cost of producing a business letter is increasing every year. Most business firms are desperately seeking ways to reduce costs. In fact, the single most important factor in bringing about the transition to word processing and eventual office automation is sharply-rising costs.

A senior industrial economist at Stanford Research Institute points out that "the current recession has brought a real awareness by companies that they have to identify and control office costs and improve productivity."[6] Word processing equipment is one means by which management can reduce costs, because money invested in these machines works to lower the cost of the human labor needed for paperwork. Capital investment in labor-saving equipment for each office worker now runs about $2,000 annually, in comparison with $25,000 spent for each manufacturing employee. By 1985, the amount spent annually for each office worker is expected to increase to $10,000 or more. The number of word processing typewriters in use is expected to double before 1980.[7] Dictation machines, also an essential part of word processing systems, can considerably improve the efficiency and productivity of both management and clerical staff. Modern machine technology, however, is not the sole solution to the problem of productivity.

---

[4] "Business Letter Cost Up Again," *Management World* (July 1976), p. 34.

[5] *Occupational Manpower and Training Needs*, U.S. Department of Labor, Bureau of Labor Statistics, Bulletin 1824 (1974), p. 12.

[6] "The Office of the Future," *op. cit.*, p. 49.

[7] *Ibid.*, p. 53.

THE HUMAN ELEMENT
IN WORD PROCESSING

New work methods and equipment will require changes in traditional work relationships, like the one-to-one relationship of a business executive to a secretary; and changing work habits may prove the biggest stumbling block to office automation. The president of the company which manufactures the Redactron automatic typewriter, states, "It always takes longer than we expect to change the way people customarily do their business. The EDP industry in the 1950s thought that the whole world would have made the transition to computers by 1960. And it hasn't happened yet."[8] Nevertheless, computers, electronic data processing, and word processing are here to stay. Most experts agree that automated office systems are not far off and that word processing is the most likely means for bringing them about. Case studies indicate that a start is already being made to combine word processing and data processing. These efforts—together with new advances in telecommunications and records management—may produce the long-awaited total management information system (MIS).

If word processing successfully effects a transition to the automated office of the future, human behavior rather than modern technology will be the deciding factor. Office workers at every level, from top management down to office clerk, must understand the need for improved productivity. They must overcome resistance to change in their work habits and in their relationships with fellow workers. At the executive level, for example, a corporation president may have to face the loss of a private secretary outside the office door. Even worse, he or she may be forced to learn how to dictate to a machine and to share the services of an administrative secretary with several other executives. At the same time, secretaries may find that specialization of tasks leads to professionalization and promotion on the basis of individual ability and work performance, rather than on the standing of their bosses in the office hierarchy.

Shortages of skilled personnel and changing social attitudes are also contributing to the need to improve office productivity. As more women in business demand equal opportunity with men, larger numbers will enter the management field and fewer will settle for clerical positions. Word processing, as an automated, cost-controlled approach to quality production of office paperwork, provides one new career opportunity for women, leading possibly to supervisory or management positions.

By 1985, half the nation's workers will be in white-collar jobs. The Bureau of Labor Statistics projects a total of 53.7 million persons employed as white-collar workers by then. Included in this category are clerks and secretaries, managers and administrators, professionals (law-

---

[8] *Ibid.*, p. 48.

yers, doctors, educators, CPA's, architects, and others), technical workers (engineers, draftsmen, computer experts, and others), and sales personnel (travel agents, insurance agents, real estate brokers, automobile salesmen, and others). These people are involved in office work in varying degrees, and these are the people directly affected by word processing.

Computer technology and electronic equipment have already made significant changes in American life and work habits. Perhaps the most exciting prospect in the coming decade is the challenge offered by further changes within the office environment, both for those already in white-collar jobs and for newcomers entering the field. These two groups make up a sizable segment of the population. To understand the modern business world, these people—particularly those in middle and top management—must understand word processing (WP), electronic data processing (EDP), the systems approach to office management, computers, and management information systems (MIS). These concepts will be discussed in the chapters that follow.

When a dynamic new business concept is introduced and receives rapid acceptance, as word processing has done, any attempt at a written description faces the danger of becoming out of date even before publication. One way of overcoming this hazard is to limit the description to a specific time period. This book attempts to present an overall view of the word processing concept, from its introduction to the present, in terms of equipment, procedures, and personnel, and in relation to the concept of a total automated office system. Having acquired this background information, you should try to keep yourself up to date by reading the latest journal articles and by visiting, when possible, nearby installations and demonstrations of new equipment. In order to understand word processing, you must become familiar with the many new words and phrases connected with this subject. For this reason, a glossary is included at the back of the book.

SUGGESTED READINGS

"Business Letter Costs Up Again," *Management World*, July 1976, pp. 34–35.

Dartnell's Glossary of Word Processing Terms. Chicago: The Dartnell Corporation, 1975.

HANNA, J. MARSHALL, ESTELLE L. POPHAM, RITA SLOAN TILTON. "Part 2. Word Processing—Typewriting, Copying and Duplicating," *Secretarial Procedures and Administration*. Sixth Edition, Cincinnati: South-Western Publishing Co., 1973.

KLEINSCHROD, WALTER A. *Management's Guide to Word Processing*. Chicago: The Dartnell Corporation, 1975.

Occupational Manpower and Training Needs. Washington, D.C.: Department of Labor, Bureau of Labor Statistics, Bulletin 1824, 1974.

"The Office of the Future," *Business Week*, June 30, 1975, pp. 48–84.

Chapter 2

THE DEVELOPMENT OF WORD PROCESSING EQUIPMENT

AUTOMATIC TYPEWRITERS AND MODERN WORD PROCESSING

The origins of modern word processing and the automatic typewriter date back to the early 1960's, when International Business Machines Corporation (IBM) introduced the **Selectric** typewriter. The Selectric was radically different from standard electric typewriters. IBM developed the machine originally as a computer printout terminal. The Selectric's outstanding feature is a spinning, "golfball" element containing type. (See Figure 2–1.) Unlike a standard typewriter, in which the paper carriage moves each time a key is struck, the Selectric has no moving carriage. As the keyboard is fingered by the typist, the type ball moves across the surface of the paper, spinning around to present the proper character. Elimination of the heavy moving carriage permits vastly improved typing speeds. On a Selectric, the speed of a good typist can increase up to 50 percent.

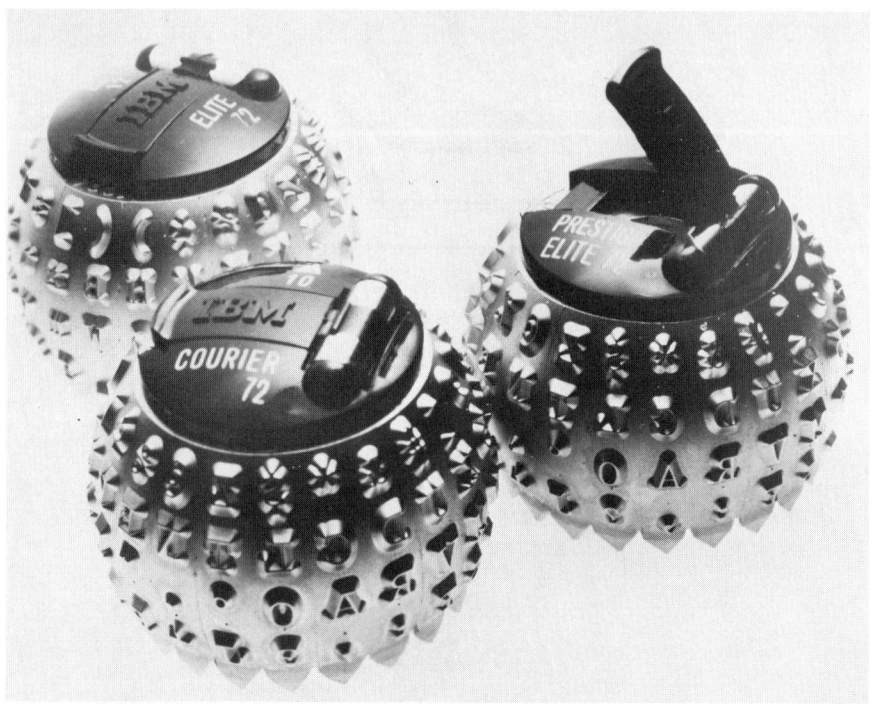

FIGURE 2-1
IBM Selectric element.

In 1964, IBM added a magnetic tape-editing device to the Selectric, and, in the process, provided the machine with a memory capability. Basically, the **Magnetic Tape Selectric Typewriter (MT/ST)** is an electric typewriter wired to a tape recorder. As the typist strokes the keys at rough-draft speed, the typed material is recorded simultaneously on the paper in the machine and on a magnetic tape mounted on a changeable cartridge. Text can be revised and errors corrected simply by backspacing and typing over the information to be changed. Automatically, the revised information is stored in place of the original. Stored typing on tape can be located automatically by the machine, which scans tape at the rate of 900 characters a second. At the push of a button, the MT/ST types out error-free finished documents from the stored characters on the tape, at speeds of 180 words a minute, or three times the speed of a human typist. If the typist codes the magnetic tape with instructions for the machine to stop at certain points, variable information (such as names or numbers) can be typed in by hand. Thereafter, the machine adjusts word spacing and line endings to the manual insertions and continues typing stored information from the tape.

The MT/ST was conceived as an automatic device for the repetitive typing of letters in volume, with little or no human intervention except for a typist's inserting paper and variable data into the machine as required. However, the machine's text editing capability made the MT/ST an unexpected success. A letter or long document need be typed in full only once since corrections, deletions, and revisions are possible without retyping the entire text. Secretarial productivity is consequently greatly increased. By the late 1960s, sales of the MT/ST exceeded expectations, and IBM began to realize it had something distinctive to market.

The term "word processing" or *Textverarbeitung* was first used in Germany in 1965 by IBM's sales staff. It was adopted gradually in this country by IBM's office products division to describe their multiproduct sales line. "Word processing" was a useful concept that enabled IBM salespeople to talk to prospective customers in an overall way about various kinds of dictation equipment and typewriter models.

The chief problem with the MT/ST machine, which is no longer built by IBM although still available under leasing agreements, is its complexity of operation. The typist requires training to a high level of proficiency in order to understand the tape and to manipulate the machine to best advantage. The typist must be able to "think tape"; this requires considerable concentration. Revisions often take more time than simply retyping the material from scratch. As a way of making the machine easier to operate and more practical for general office correspondence, IBM substituted magnetic cards for the tape and, in 1969, introduced another model, the **Magnetic Card Selectric Typewriter (MC/ST)**, followed by the **Mag Card II** (Figure 2–2), and the latest model, the **Mag Card/A** (Figure 2–3).

IBM's Mag Card II is currently the most widely used word processing machine. The Mag Card II's electronic "memory" holds up to 8,000 characters or about 2½ average-length pages of typed material. The magnetic cards are used exclusively for storage of the text, which can be inserted or deleted in the machine's memory. The machine has dual pitch, which makes possible a merging operation, using material from two or more magnetic cards to produce a single document. For instance, one card may contain a list of names and addresses and another the body of a letter, or a series of cards may each contain a single paragraph of a letter. When inserted into the machine, the text contained on the cards is typed out in finished form as a complete letter or document. The versatility of the machine accounts in large part for its popularity.

Because of protective legal patents and the intricate technology of the Selectric machine, IBM had the automatic typewriter market all to itself until the late 1960s. Smaller manufacturers of automatic typing systems, who lacked the research facilities and financial capacity of IBM, were forced to base their system designs around the Selectric, even though

FIGURE 2-2
At the offices of TIAA-CREF, a nonprofit insurance company, paragraphs prerecorded on magnetic cards are inserted into the IBM Mag Card II and played out in appropriate sequence to produce a customized, error-free letter. For details, see Chapter 6.

they incorporated their own distinctive editing and memory devices. In the early 1970s, however, Selectric-based text-editing machines were brought to the automatic typewriter market by Wang Laboratories, Redactron Corporation, Savin Business Machines, CPT Corporation, Sperry Remington, Trendata, Ty-Data, and Quindata.

One exception to the Selectric-based machine was Olivetti's S-14 "Mastermind." An easy-to-operate, flexible editing machine, the Olivetti uses computer-style magnetic tape cartridges. A cartridge provides a storage capacity of 250,000 characters or approximately 150 pages of typed text, as well as an excellent information retrieval system for locating stored text.

FIGURE 2-3
IBM Mag Card/A.

In 1974, Xerox Corporation introduced a new automated typing system based on original technology. The Xerox 800 electronic typing system features a unique, electronically driven print wheel that contains one type character on each spoke of the wheel (Figure 2-4 and 2-5). As with IBM's golfball element, the Xerox print wheel is changeable and comes in a variety of type styles. The most important difference between the two machines is in the playback speed, with the Xerox 800 offering 350 words a minute compared with IBM's 180 words a minute. Despite its recent arrival in the marketplace, however, the Xerox 800 is basically the same type of stand-alone automatic typewriter as the original word processing machines introduced by IBM in the 1960s—the MT/ST and the MC/ST.

FIGURE 2-4
Xerox typing wheel.

FIGURE 2-5
The Xerox 800 Electronic Typing System automatically types from magnetic tapes or cards in either a single or a dual unit. The model shown above is a dual tape cassette unit, capable of turning out error-free documents at a rate of up to 350 words a minute. The Xerox print wheel can be changed in seconds and is available in a wide range of type styles.

COMMUNICATING TYPEWRITERS

A different variation of the MC/ST was introduced by IBM in 1971 in the form of the Communicating Mag Card Selectric typewriter, or the CMC. Originally planned as an input device to computer memories, the CMC was sold instead primarily for communications between word processors. The CMC is capable of transmitting typewritten copy to another CMC over telephone lines, either locally or long distance. When connected to a computer, the CMC operates as a terminal, entering or receiving communications in either a word processing or a data processing system.

The CMC also has the capability of communicating with any TWX or Telex terminal in the world and with other makes of communicating typewriters. Its top transmission speed is 15 characters per second. Western Union's TWX and Telex services are used by business firms. They operate over telephone lines connecting two teletypists, who carry on a conversation by typing back and forth. Instead of vocal messages, the result is a written record of the messages exchanged. The TWX teletypewriter transmits 10 characters per second; and the Telex teleprinter, 7 characters per second.

In 1976, Xerox introduced a communicating model of the Xerox 800 that receives information over telephone lines at speeds up to 120 characters per second, or eight times faster than most competitive systems. The Xerox 800 communicating electronic typing system is available in single or dual magnetic tape models and can be leased or purchased. Lease prices range from about $300 to $400 a month; purchase price is approximately $14,000 for single tape and dual tape models.

Redactron's Redactor communicating typewriter can transmit a 30-page newsletter to another Redactor in three minutes. The Redactor can also transmit via computer, telephone, TWX, or Telex in four communication modes: high speed batch, conversational, TWX, and Telex. (See Glossary for a definition of these two terms.) Wang's 1220 TC, on the other hand, communicates only with like machines and computers at speeds up to 150 characters per second on tape. (See Figure 2-6.)

SECOND-GENERATION CRT OR MICROCOMPUTER WORD PROCESSING SYSTEMS

Newer entries to the word processing market are the more expensive and more sophisticated CRT (cathode ray tube) systems that display text on an electronic video screen as it is typed. This process eliminates the need for paper when typing first drafts. A CRT machine is, in fact, a microcomputer word processing system, since it is built around a microprocessor (which is more fully described in Chapter 7). Because of this microprocessor, CRT systems tend to have larger memory capabilities than the first-generation typewriter-based systems. Consequently, text can be more heavily changed and edited, a feature particularly useful in law firms and other organizations which commonly produce lengthy documents requiring heavy editing and revision, such as leases, contracts, wills and trusts, reports, manuals, specifications, and financial statements. The CRT microcomputer systems also have the potential for communicating with other computer word processing systems and with communicating typewriters, a topic discussed in greater detail in later chapters.

Second-Generation CRT or Microcomputer Word Processing Systems

CRT microcomputer systems consist basically of a video-display terminal with an electronic keyboard for input and editing, and a separate printer for the output of documents. Magnetic tape cassettes or disks are used as storage devices. The printout units commonly used with the CRTs, the Diablo and the Qume printers, are faster than the Selectric. The Diablo prints out typewriter-quality finished text from cassettes or disks, or from stored data, at speeds of 350 words a minute; and the Qume prints out at 525 words a minute. The printer operates independently from the keyboard terminal. Therefore, the operator can continue to enter or edit text on the video-display terminal while the printer types out previously entered material in finished form.

FIGURE 2-6
Wang Laboratories System 1200 Cassette Typewriter can be used with an optional CRT attachment. The Model 1220 Dual Cassette System illustrated, features an inexpensive and removable magnetic tape cassette capable of storing between 30 and 40 pages of text. Controls for editing and revising text material are located on either side of the typewriter keyboard.

CRT or video-display terminals have been used in larger computer systems for the past ten years. Their introduction in the microcomputer word processing systems may result in their becoming the most popular of all word processing systems. Research has shown that the video-display terminals, which operate silently at instantaneous electronic speed, are an ideal medium for human operators. As the typist fingers the silent electronic keyboard of the terminal, the text appears instantly in clear view on the screen at eye level. Errors can be corrected on sight. When the typist is satisfied with the text on display, a simple push of a button places it in storage or requests a printout. The instantaneous rapport between the typist and the video-display frequently results in a doubling of work output.

In a recent three-month test and evaluation of electronic word processing equipment, the Congressional Research Service (CRS), a department of the Library of Congress in Washington, D.C., settled on the cathode ray tube approach. CRS found that the CRT unit produced the most work in the shortest time and for the least cost per 1000 keystrokes in their test application. In addition, the CRT system required a fraction of the training time necessary in the typewriter-based systems, and the productivity of typists was immediately higher.[1]

Several manufacturers market CRT microcomputer systems. One of the current leaders in the field, Lexitron Corporation, produces the Videotype Text Processor. Another manufacturer is Vydec, Inc. (Vydec is jointly owned by Exxon Corporation, Hewlett-Packard, and Vydec's top management team.) Introduced in 1974, the Vydec machine has a unit price of approximately $16,000. Both Lexitron and Vydec machines were designed from the start to be text processors, unlike a third machine, manufactured by Linolex Systems, Inc. (See Figure 2–7.)

Linolex equipment was originally designed as computer terminals and data entry devices. Later it developed into word processing equipment. Linolex equipment is generally broader in capability and more expensive than either Lexitron or Vydec. Linolex is a subsidiary of 3M Company, and the machine is known as the 3M Linolex Video Text Editor.

Stand-alone (that is, self-contained) word processing systems, whether first-generation typewriter-based or second-generation microcomputer-based, are economically feasible for most business firms because the initial investment can be paid for in two to three years from reduced salary costs alone. Therefore, stand-alone units are expected to continue being the workhorses of word processing operations and to predominate in small offices.

---

[1] "Library of Congress Steps into Word Processing," *Government Executive* (July 1975).

FIGURE 2-7
The new 3M Linolex Video Text Editor is a word processing unit with a cathode ray tube (CRT) display. A keyed text is recorded on a magnetic storage device called a diskette, similar in size to a 45 RPM record. Diskettes are stored conveniently, with each diskette capable of carrying 75 pages of material.

The ultimate in word processing, however, is the computer-based system. For actual word and/or text processing, a standard computer-based system (or, to a lesser extent, a minicomputer-based system) is unbeatable for storage capacity, speed of output, sophistication, and flexibility. The vast difference in cost and volume of work required to justify its use places computer word processing in a class by itself. For that reason, computer and minicomputer word processing systems will be discussed as a separate topic in Chapter 7.

IMPORTANCE OF DICTATION EQUIPMENT IN WORD PROCESSING

Desktop and portable dictation machines have been around for many decades but have usually been regarded by business executives as optional rather than required office equipment. In general, executives and their secretaries prefer face-to-face dictating. Whenever possible, they avoid using machines for dictation. The introduction of automatic typewriters and modern word processing, however, makes the use of dictation equipment essential. On a cost basis alone, it makes little sense to purchase a $10,000 typewriter or rent one for $250 a month and then let it stand idle while a secretary sits in the boss's office taking or waiting to take shorthand.

The traditional secretary with a standard electric typewriter normally produces about 100 lines of mailable typed copy each day. Typing takes up about one-third of the secretary's day, with two-thirds of the day spent on dictation, answering phones, and other tasks. However, a word processing secretary, using a magnetic keyboard, must produce a minimum of 600 lines of finished copy a day just to maintain a lower cost-per-line ratio than that of the traditional secretary using a standard machine.[2] A cost-conscious company executive can hardly request a secretary to stop operating such an expensive automatic machine simply to take dictation, particularly when the option of a dictating machine exists. It is also incongruous to expect the user of this sophisticated typing equipment to waste time in deciphering handwritten drafts and revisions. Changes in the cost of secretarial equipment require changes in office procedures and work organization.

Equally important in the cost is the fact that the productivity of the word originator is greatly enhanced by machine dictation, thus allowing time for other work.[3] When word originators understand the benefits to themselves and their organization, they are more strongly motivated to experiment with dictation equipment, particularly with short letters and memoranda. Even when machines are difficult to use, as in the case of lengthy, complex reports, the author's secretary can when necessary take dictation and then redictate the shorthand notes into a machine. The notes are thus converted into a medium that permits other secretaries to transcribe them. The possibility of redirecting work from one secretary to another by the use of dictation equipment enables the office staff to cope with peak workloads. The word originator benefits by

---

[2] S. J. Kalow, "Word Processing," *Words* (Autumn 1975), p. 14.

[3] Paul G. Truax, "The Microphone vs. the Pencil," *Word Processing* (September/October 1974), p. 14.

the speed with which dictation is converted into typed drafts or final form and returned for further revision or signature.[4]

Dictation equipment and automatic typewriters are both essential to modern word processing systems. Just as shorthand required the invention of the typewriter and its development for office use before coming into prominence at the turn of the century, so too dictation equipment required the invention of the automatic typewriter and the development of word processing systems.

CENTRALIZED DICTATION EQUIPMENT— DISCRETE MEDIA

A variety of recording media is used in dictation equipment: magnetic belts, magnetic disks, and magnetic tapes enclosed in cassettes or cartridges. The introduction of new centralized dictation equipment using these discrete or separate units of recording media has tremendously expanded the potential efficiency of word processing systems in recent years. One feature these new products have in common is an automatic changer. **An automatic changer permits the continuous central recording of dictation without the need for constantly changing the recording medium.** The recording medium provides anywhere from six minutes to ninety minutes of recording time and is used in portable and desk-top models as well as in centralized dictation equipment. When a word originator finishes dictating, the medium must be removed from the recorder by hand. Thereafter, a transcriptionist inserts the belt, disk, or tape into a separate transcribing unit. As the medium plays out, the transcriptionist listens and simultaneously types the recorded words. A long letter or report may require two or more belts, disks, cassettes, or cartridges. The efficiency of these removable or **discrete media** dictation machines is greatly enhanced when an automatic changer makes possible long periods of dictation without the need for human intervention. The use of cassettes and cartridges, as opposed to belts or disks, also simplifies handling.

The first entry into the automatic changer market was Lanier's Tel-Edisette System, introduced in 1973 (Figure 2–8). The Tel-Edisette uses twelve standard cassettes, which have a total recording capability of six to nine hours. The system features two modes of operation. Normal mode ejects cassettes when they are filled with dictation and automatically inserts fresh ones. Priority mode permits the person dictating to eject a cassette for immediate transcription. The essential components of the machine are a desk phone input unit, a twelve-cassette central recorder, and a transcribing unit. According to individual requirements,

---

[4] *Ibid.*, pp. 14–17.

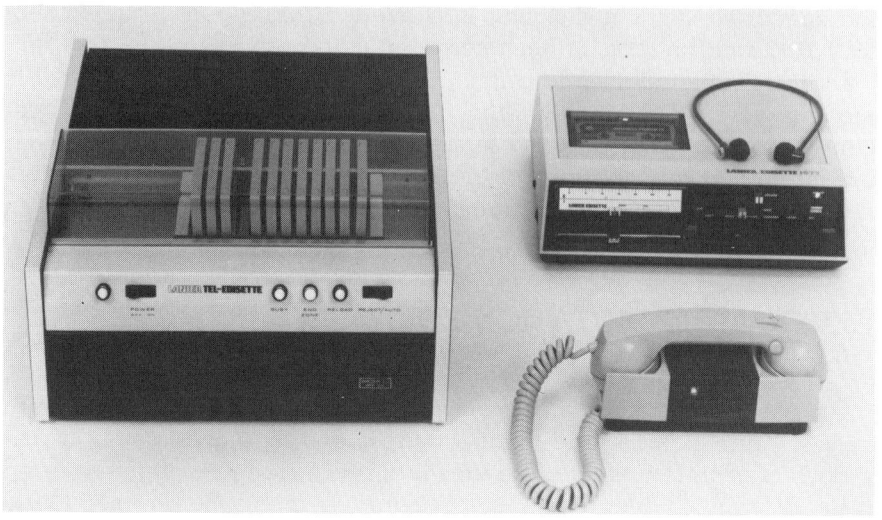

FIGURE 2-8
Lanier Tel-Edisette is a central dictating system composed of a desk phone input unit, a 12-cassette central recorder with an automatic cassette changer and up to 9 hours recording capacity, and a transcribing unit. Existing internal or external telephones can be used for input with recorder operation completely controlled by dialing different numbers internally or with the pushbuttons on Touch-Tone telephones.

additional units can be interconnected to provide increased word processing capacity. Existing internal or external telephones can be used for input. Recorder operation is completely controlled by dialing different numbers internally or with the pushbuttons on Touch-Tone telephones. This type of system permits telephone dictation from any dial or Touch-Tone phone anywhere in the world. Once the recording is received, the cassettes can be easily distributed to transcriptionists, sent to other areas for off-premise typing, or stored. The Tel-Edisette Recorder unit is priced at approximately $1,500.

In 1975, Philips/Norelco's 260 Automatic Dictation System was introduced. (See Figure 2-9.) The recording capacity of the 260 is the same as that of the Tel-Edisette, six hours. But the 260 uses minicassettes, each of which accepts fifteen minutes of dictation. It works on *voice operated relay* **(VOR)**, *a device that activates the recorder when voice sounds come in over a telephone line and automatically stops the medium after five seconds of silence to eliminate the recording of silence.* The basic recorder unit costs approximately $2,500.

IBM introduced a new dictation system in 1975—the 6:5 Cartridge System—which uses magnetic disks instead of belts. Each disk holds up to six minutes of dictation or two average typed pages; each cartridge holds up to 25 disks; each recorder holds two cartridges, for a maximum

Centralized Dictation Equipment—Discrete Media 25

overall recording time of five hours. The IBM system is designed with work distribution in mind, since special material and overloads can be easily sorted and the disks distributed among several transcriptionists. Various configurations, from desktop to remote microphone or telephone system, are possible. The system's modular design makes it adaptable and expandable. The basic 6:5 system (microphone, recorder, and transcriber) costs approximately $1,500.

The Sony Remote Dictation System is also compatible with any telephone switchboard and, once installed, provides a full-function dictation machine on everyone's desk by means of the telephone. The basic system consists of the Sony BM-35 cassette dictation machine, using standard cassettes, with up to 45 minutes on each side, and a remote

FIGURE 2-9
The Philips/Norelco 260 Automatic Dictation System utilizes 24 miniature, reusable, self-contained "idea capsules" in an automatic changer unit. Blank spaces are avoided due to voice-controlled operation. Transcription workload scheduling is accomplished directly from the Norelco 260. A built-in intercom permits direct communication between dictator and supervisor. Visual and audible indicators provide rapid access to priority dictation.

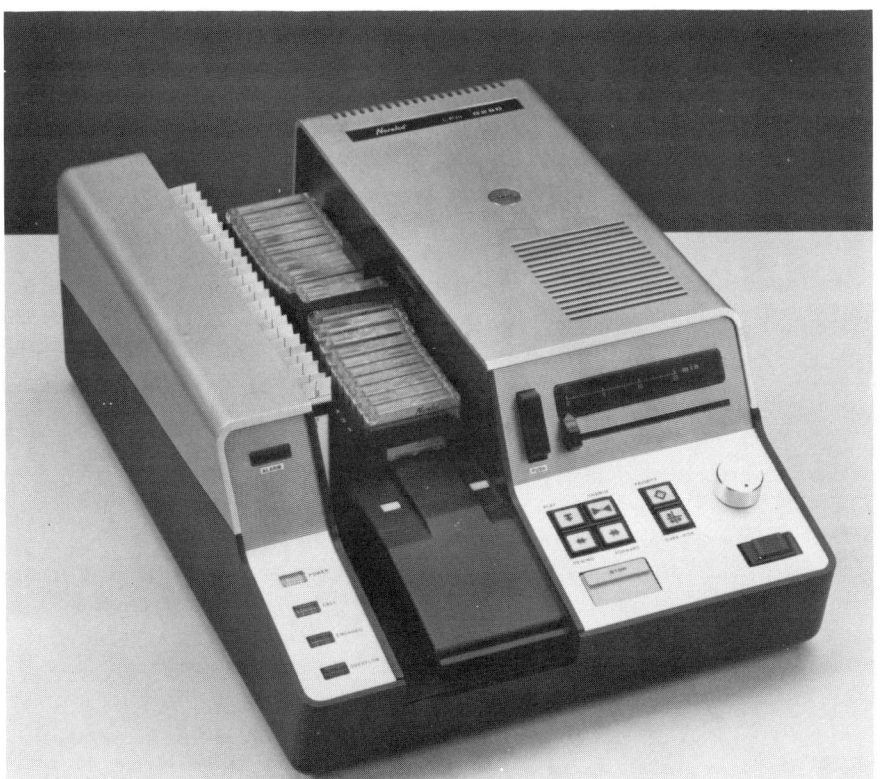

dictation unit. For continuous, extended dictation time, additional units can be added. When a cassette is filled on one machine, the person dictating is automatically switched to another. Sony features a complete indexing system. Visual and electronic indexing inform the transcriptionist of the number of documents on each cassette and the length of each.

CENTRALIZED DICTATION EQUIPMENT— ENDLESS LOOP

The *endless loop or "tank type" recorders* **are** *continuous flow systems* that have several advantages over discrete media equipment. The tape is sealed in a tank. Since it loops around constantly, there is no need to remove it or even to touch the recorder. In fact, the recorder equipment is usually stored in an out-of-the-way office area. Another advantage is that the transcriptionist can start to play back dictation while the person dictating continues to feed in material. In an endless loop tank, playback can begin just down the tape a short distance from where the person is dictating—an important feature when rush jobs are involved.

Recording capacity in the Lanier Nyematic VIP System, the first endless loop recorder, provides 100 minutes of continuous recording time, or about eight to ten hours average input. The Nyematic provides automatic unattended use, 24 hours a day. The person dictating uses a handset similar to a telephone receiver. When dictation is recorded, a light on the secretary's desk signals that action. When dictation is completely transcribed, the light goes out.

As an organization grows, unlimited expansion of the endless loop system is possible. There is no limit to the addition of input stations, and even automatic recorder selection and a supervisor's console can be added. A supervisor's console or monitoring panel contains a row of dials which indicate which tank is in use and which is idle, as well as the amount of backlog that remains to be transcribed. Endless loop systems, like discrete media systems, are used either individually by a person who generates a great deal of dictation, or centrally by many word originators in one or more departments or in an entire organization.

Dictaphone's Thought Tank System 193 is an endless loop machine equipped with an internal computer to distribute workload automatically in a word processing center. At a glance, the supervisor can monitor the center's input, output, backlog of work to be done, turnaround time for getting the work out, and the productivity rate of each secretary in the center. (See Figure 2–10.) Tape in the Dictaphone Thought Tank System has a capacity of 60 minutes of continuous recording time.

Prices for the endless loop systems depend on a number of factors in

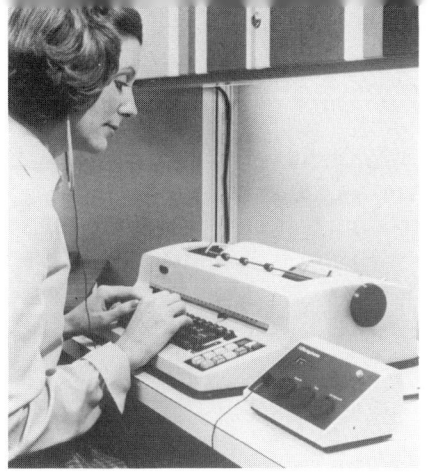 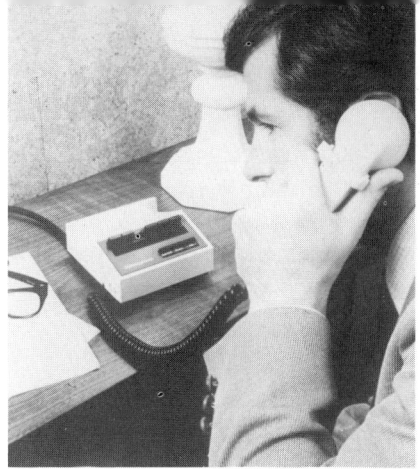

FIGURE 2-10
Dictaphone's Thought Tank System 193 has a fast forward control and an electronic autoscan that stops the recorder between dictation segments. The secretary (above left) can easily locate a document out of sequence and then return to previous dictation. Dictation from the word originator (above right) is automatically directed to the secretary who will provide the fastest turnaround time. The system's computerized controls distribute the workload and assure even turnaround time. The Word Controller console tells the supervisor (below) at a glance the center's daily input, output, backlog situation, and typists' individual output rates.

addition to the equipment itself, such as phone charges where applicable, optional **interfaces** (that is, **connections to telephone lines**), voice operated relays, and accessories. One dictation and transcription station in an individual system can range from $600 to over $1,000. In a central system, a single basic unit starts at about $1,200.

TYPES OF TELEPHONE SYSTEMS USED WITH CENTRALIZED DICTATION[5]

A number of alternative methods of dictating exist for making centralized dictation responsive to the needs of individual organizations. Desktop dictation equipment usually comes with a separate hand microphone. But the new centralized systems, whether discrete media or endless loop, employ standard desk phones for dictation. The two basic types of telephone methods for dictation are Private Wire Systems and Private Branch Exchange (PBX), which uses either dial or pushbutton phones.

1. **Private wire systems** are internal systems that use equipment purchased or rented by the organization for its exclusive use and not supplied by the local telephone company. These systems require a special telephone network in order to connect the person dictating in a private office to the central recorder located in the word processing center. With private wire systems, three kinds of equipment are available to connect the word originator with the central recorder.

   a. **Nonselector equipment.** This is connected to only one recorder. If that is in use, the word originator must wait.

   b. **Manual selector.** The word originator can select a free recorder with this equipment.

   c. **Automatic selector.** The first free recorder is automatically selected for the word originator.

   Private wire systems also have the capability for dial-in dictation and for recording messages and taking orders from any telephone anywhere.

2. **Private branch exchange (PBX) systems** connect equipment owned by the telephone company with the centralized dictation equipment made by various vendors. (See Chapter 8 for more details.) This eliminates the need for a separate handset, since the desk telephone is used for dictating. Two kinds of connection are available—a recorder coupler or a trunk link interface. A recorder coupler is less expensive but does not interpret dial or tone signals to command the dictation equipment. Trunk links permit telephone equipment to decode both dial

---

[5] Source: "Telephonic Alternatives for Central Dictation," *Word Processing World* (May/June 1975).

FIGURE 2-11   A TYPICAL CENTRAL DICTATION SYSTEM

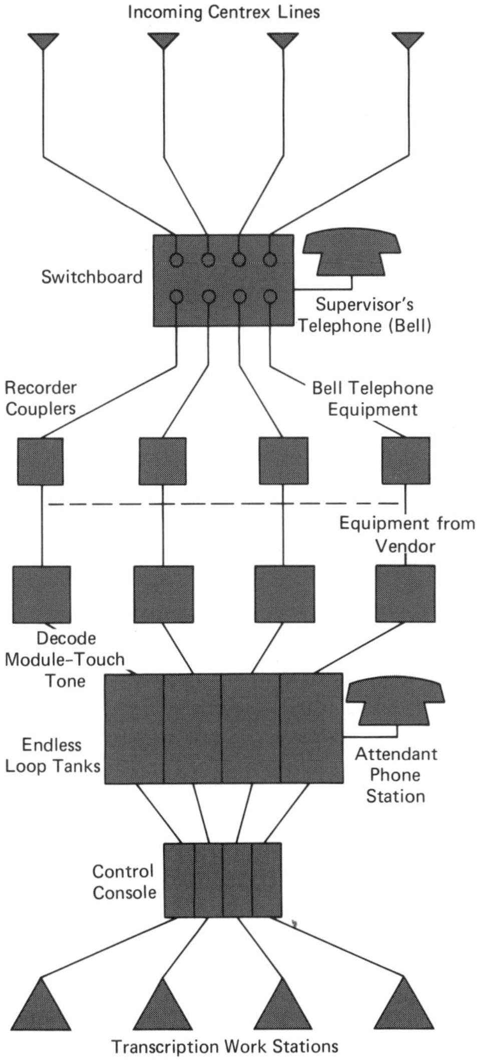

A typical PBX central dictation system built around the use of endless loop tanks involves equipment from both the telephone company and the dictating vendor. The telephone company supplies the telephone, switchboard, and interface (recorder coupler). The manufacturer supplies the decode module, tanks, control console, and transcribing equipment.

Source: "Telephonic Alternatives For Central Dictation," *Word Processing World*, May-June 1975, p. 17.

signals and Touch-Tone pushbutton signals to give instructions to the centralized dictation system. This gives the person dictating complete facilities for record, rewind, listen, and correct instructions while dictating from an internal office phone or from an external dial or Touch-Tone phone anywhere in the world. Figure 2-11 illustrates the connecting links and equipment in a typical PBX central dictation system.

Now that the basic word processing equipment and its capabilities have been described, the next chapter deals with the reasons why large and small companies are investing money in these machines and taking an office systems approach to the initiation and production of typed documents of all kinds. As previously mentioned in Chapter 1, a systems approach deals with office procedures, personnel, and equipment as an organized whole in order to achieve increased output and reduced costs. Chapter 3 describes the effects of sophisticated word processing equipment on office personnel and procedures.

SUGGESTED READINGS

KALOW, S.J. "Word Processing," *Words*, Vol. 4, No. 3, Autumn 1975, pp. 14-15.

"Library of Congress Steps into Word Processing," *Government Executive*, Vol. 7, No. 7, July 1975.

STERNIN, BERNARD. "The New World of Mag Card II," *The Practical Lawyer*, January 15, 1976, pp. 21-32.

"Telephonic Alternatives for Central Dictation," *Word Processing World*, Vol. 2, No. 3, May-June 1975, p. 17.

TRUAX, PAUL G. "The Microphone vs. the Pencil," *Word Processing*, September/October 1974, pp. 14-17.

Chapter

WORD PROCESSING SYSTEMS - THEORY AND DEVELOPMENT

A SYSTEMS APPROACH TO OFFICE PAPERWORK

A systems approach to office paperwork production regards workers, work procedures, and office equipment as an organized whole. Each component is considered not as a separate entity in itself, but rather as it relates to the whole office system. The goal of a systems approach is the performance of work tasks by everyone in the office in the most efficient manner, at the least cost, and in the fastest time possible. This approach in combination with electronic computers proved successful in industry in the 1960s, when cost-saving automation was introduced to accounting offices and to factory operations. At the same time, changes were made in work procedures. Many clerical positions in filing, payroll, inventory control, and customer billing were eliminated. However, large numbers of clerical workers were needed as keypunch operators and digital computer operators, positions created by the new computers and the field of electronic data processing (EDP). Similarly, the introduction of electronic word processing equipment in the executive office is now bringing about changes in white-collar jobs and work procedures, creating new positions, and altering or eliminating old ones.

Although word processing equipment was first introduced in the 1960s, the need for utilizing its cost-saving features did not become urgent until the economic recession and inflation in the early 1970s. A recent survey by the Stanford Research Institute indicates that, while office costs formerly represented 20 to 30 percent of the total company cost, today they represent 40 to 50 percent of the total.[1] The computer revolution of the 1960s was the impetus for an information explosion which tremendously increased the flood of office paperwork. In the past five years, a systems approach to office operations, incorporating the new word processing technology, has become the accepted solution of about 15 percent of all the companies in the United States.

WORD PROCESSING AND WORD PROCESSING SYSTEMS DEFINED

The terms **word processing** and **word processing system** are frequently used interchangeably, thus causing some confusion. The terms are not identical in meaning and need clarification. *Dartnell's Glossary of Word Processing Terms* defines **word processing** broadly as **the automation of document production** and more specifically as **the combination of people, procedures, and equipment that transforms ideas into printed communications and helps facilitate the flow of related office work.** However, a **word processing system** is defined as **a combination of equipment and personnel working in an environment of job specialization and supervisory controls for the purpose of producing typed documents in a routinized, cost-effective manner.** Thus, job specialization and supervisory controls are key features of a word processing system.

For secretaries in a word processing system to produce typed documents in a routinized, cost-effective manner, secretarial duties must be divided into two broad areas of specialization—typing and nontyping. The traditional work of a secretary is divided into two new positions— one designated as a word processing or correspondence secretary, and the other designated as an administrative secretary. The former is responsible for the typing function and the latter for the nontyping functions. In a word processing system, input may be either from a principal who is an executive or an administrative secretary on behalf of a princi-

---

[1] "The Office of the Future," *Business Week* (June 30, 1975), p. 49.

Word Processing and Word Processing Systems Defined

FIGURE 3-1 THE WORD PROCESSING SYSTEM

1. The Word Originator

Modes of Origination
- Longhand
- Steno
- Machine Dictation—
  Cartridge, Disk or Belt—
  Desk Systems
  Central Systems
  Tank or Endless Loop—
  Individual Systems
  Central Systems

Original Input or Back for Corrections

3. Typing (Copying)

Typewriter Alternatives
- "Regular" Electrics or Standards
- Automatic Models
- Mechanical Text Editing Machines
- Multi-station Systems—Time Shared
- CRT Editing Machines

2. *Methods of Delivery*
- Personal
- Messenger
- PBX
- Dial Systems ⎫
- Private Wire ⎬ Machine Dictation Options
- Telephone   ⎪
  Re-transmission to a Center
- Facsimile   ⎭

5. Out to Be—
- Mailed, Filed, Hand Delivered
- Copied, Duplicated, Distributed

4. Back for Review

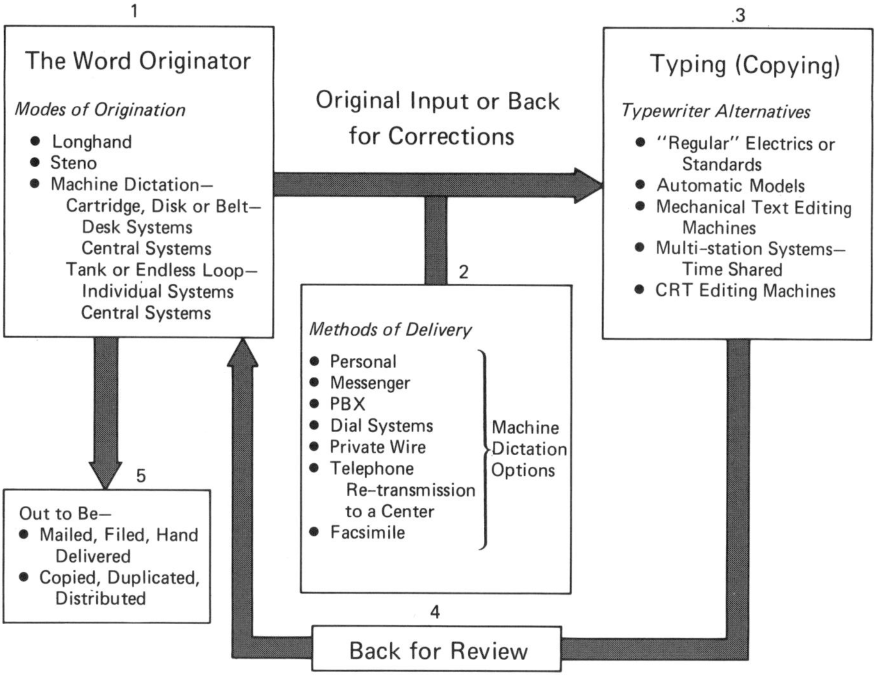

Source: Walter A. Kleinschrod. *Management's Guide to Word Processing.* Chicago: The Dartnell Corporation, 1975.

pal, since both are considered word originators. Output is by a word processing or correspondence secretary, who is a typing specialist or technician. Both kinds of secretaries usually perform work for two or more executives and come under the supervision of a word processing supervisor. Figure 3–1 diagrams a word processing system.

The traditional secretary who works for one executive, who uses an automatic typewriter, and who also handles nontyping tasks is involved in word processing but *not* necessarily in a word processing system. For a word processing system to be efficient, secretarial labor must be divided, and a secretary must usually work for more than one executive. The orientation of this book is toward the automation of secretarial work by means of word processing systems, which represents a radical departure from traditional secretarial work. In theory, word processing systems separate production typing from administrative chores. The traditional secretary is replaced by two new kinds of secretaries. The word processing or correspondence secretary is an expert machine technician. The administrative secretary is a qualified assistant, responsible for the mail, telephones, and files, who is also free to handle special projects for more than one principal. The new work-flow pattern resulting from a word processing system effects radical changes in office procedures and interpersonal relationships, upsetting traditional work habits and role concepts for both executives and secretaries.

TRADITIONAL SECRETARIAL POSITIONS

In order to understand the processes involved in the automation of secretarial work, we must consider the tasks traditionally performed by workers in the secretarial field. In 1974, approximately 35 percent of all employed women in the United States held clerical jobs. More than 4 million of these women were typists, stenographers, and secretaries. These three positions, each of which is distinguished by specific work tasks, also represent different levels in the traditional career ladder for aspiring executive secretaries.

Typists, stenographers, and secretaries are at the center of communications within their offices, and their work efforts permit the rapid flow of written information essential to office operations. Following is a brief description of these clerical occupations, from the Bureau of Labor Statistics of the Department of Labor.[2]

> TYPISTS. Beginner typists usually type headings on form letters, copy directly from handwritten drafts, and address envelopes; experienced typists handle work that requires a high degree of accuracy and independent judgment. Senior typists work from rough drafts which are difficult to read or which contain technical material. They may plan and type complicated statistical tables, combine and rearrange materials from different sources, or prepare master copies to be reproduced on copying machines. Clerk typists combine typing with filing, sorting mail, answering telephones, and other general office work. Transcribing machine operators or transcriptionists type letters and reports as they listen to dictation recorded on magnetic tape. Other typists with special duties include policy writers in insurance companies, waybill clerks in railway offices, and mortgage clerks in banks.

> For most jobs, 40 to 50 words a minute typing speed is required. In 1974, about 1 million persons worked as typists—97 per cent of them were women. They were employed throughout the entire economy, with over half of them in factories, banks, insurance companies, real estate firms, and government agencies. However, the largest single concentration of typists is found in federal, state, and local government agencies. Many thousands of job openings are expected to occur for typists in the next decade due to growth of the occupation and the need for replacements.

> STENOGRAPHERS. Stenographers take dictation and then transcribe their notes on a typewriter. They may either take shorthand or use a steno-

---

[2] From the *Occupational Outlook Handbook, 1976–1977 Edition*. U.S. Department of Labor, Bureau of Labor Statistics, Bulletin 1875.

type machine which prints symbols as certain keys are pressed. General stenographers take routine dictation and do other office tasks such as typing, filing, answering telephones, and operating office machines. Experienced and highly skilled stenographers take difficult dictation and do more responsible clerical work. They may sit in on staff meetings and give a summary report or a word-for-word record of the proceedings. They also supervise other stenographers, typists, and clerical workers. Technical stenographers must know the terms used in a particular profession, such as the medical, legal, scientific, and engineering fields. Some experienced stenographers take dictation in foreign languages, while others work as public stenographers serving traveling business people and others.

Shorthand reporters are specialized stenographers who record all statements made in a proceeding. Nearly half of them work as court reporters attached to courts of law at different levels of government. They take down all statements made at legal proceedings and present their record as the official transcript. Other shorthand reporters work as free-lance reporters who record out-of-court testimony for attorneys, meetings and conventions, and other private activities. Still others record the proceedings in the Congress of the United States, in state legislatures, and in both state and federal agencies.

Stenographers must be able to take dictation at 110 words a minute and type 40 to 50 words a minute to qualify for federal jobs and for employment in many private firms. Employment of stenographers is expected to continue the decline of recent years. The increased use of dictation machines has severely reduced the need for office stenographers. Only about 100,000 persons worked as stenographers in 1974. In contrast, however, skilled shorthand reporters appear to have good prospects as state and federal court systems expand to handle the rising number of criminal court cases and civil lawsuits. Court reporting jobs require more than 225 words of dictation a minute, and shorthand reporters in the federal government generally must take 175 words a minute.

SECRETARIES. Most secretaries type, take shorthand, and deal with visitors to the office. They relieve their employers of routine duties so that they can work on more important matters. Their duties range from filing, routing mail, and answering telephones, to more responsible tasks such as answering letters, doing statistical research, and writing reports. Some secretaries are trained in specific skills needed in certain types of work. Medical secretaries prepare case histories and medical reports; legal secretaries do legal research and help prepare briefs and legal documents; technical secretaries assist engineers or scientists in drafting reports and research proposals. Another specialized secretary is the social secretary who arranges social functions, answers personal correspondence, and keeps the employer informed about all social activities.

About 3.3 million persons—nearly all of them women—worked in jobs requiring secretarial or stenographic skills in 1974; most were secretaries. About two thirds of them work in banks, insurance companies, real estate firms, government agencies, and other establishments providing services to the public. Most specialized secretaries and stenographers work for doctors, lawyers, and other professional people. Employers look for persons who are poised, alert, and who have pleasant personalities. Discretion, judgment, and initiative are important for the more responsible secretarial positions.

Secretaries frequently increase their skills and broaden their knowledge of their company's operations by taking courses offered by the company or by local colleges and universities. As secretaries gain knowledge and experience, they can qualify for the designation Certified Professional Secretary (CPS) by passing a series of examinations given by the National Secretaries Association International. This designation is recognized by a number of employers as the mark of achievement in the secretarial field.

THE NATURE OF SECRETARIAL WORK

Secretarial duties cover a broad range of tasks, from routine typing to acting as confidant and custodian of personal and company secrets. Secretaries usually work for one person, and some executive secretaries have secretaries of their own. Specialized secretaries earn top salaries because of their experience with medical or legal procedures and their knowledge of special terminology. For the most part, however, the position of secretary is a highly general one, and secretarial skills are easily transferred from one job to another.

Despite its variations, the position of secretary is essentially a supportive one. As defined by the National Secretaries Association, a secretary is—

> . . . an assistant to an executive, possessing mastery of office skills and ability to assume responsibility without direct supervision, who displays initiative, exercises judgment, and makes decisions within the scope of her authority.[3]

Since the scope of authority depends upon the boss, the primary duty of a secretary is to work effectively with and for the boss. A secretary's salary increases and advancement depend largely on the boss rather than on personal capabilities. Secretaries to middle management executives possess essentially the same skills as secretaries to top executives. However, if an executive is in top-level company management, that executive's secretary is usually at the top level of secretarial workers in salary and status. Proving oneself capable at an administrative assistant's level and protecting the boss from unnecessary interruptions or details enable the competent secretary to become invaluable in helping an executive increase productivity at higher creative levels.

---

[3] As quoted in J. Marshall Hanna, Estelle L. Popham, Rita Sloan Tilton, *Secretarial Procedures and Administration*. Cincinnati: South-Western Publishing Co., 1973, p. 2.

At the same time, the top-level secretary must cope in the course of the daily work with constant interruptions. Since a secretary must handle incoming and outgoing telephone calls, receive visitors to the office, and await instructions from the boss, a secretary's time belongs to others. Concentration and efficient organization of work tasks are difficult to achieve. Flexibility is an important characteristic of an executive secretary, who must meet varied and unexpected demands. Frequent interruptions prevent secretaries from working at top efficiency, just as waiting for dictation or instructions from a busy executive reduces secretarial efficiency. The one-to-one relationship of an executive to a secretary frequently means that a secretary has a heavy work load when the executive is available and a light work load when the executive is tied up in meetings, away from the office, or simply refuses to delegate authority to a secretary. These peaks and valleys in work load seriously detract from secretarial efficiency.

SECRETARIAL UTILIZATION AND INCREASING OFFICE COSTS

Although most secretaries to top executives work to full capacity, research indicates that many high-salaried secretaries working for one executive, often at a level below that of a top executive, do not utilize their time or skills to the highest potential. This underutilization often comes about because the executive to whom they are assigned does not have enough work to justify having a secretary. (Remember that the boss's *title*, not *need*, customarily determines whether a secretary is provided.) Other reasons are poor organization of work assignments for the secretary and unwillingness to delegate work that the secretary is often capable of performing.

The unevenness of work distribution and frequent peak loads of typing jobs often require executives and managers to borrow each other's secretaries to get the work done. This all too common situation causes hard feelings and inefficient service, since the secretaries believe that they are responsible to one principal only. They have little concept of the team approach for completing work assignments.

On the other hand, demand for trained secretaries is great. Since 1965 average secretarial salaries have increased over 68 percent. During the ten-year period 1965–1975, the Administrative Management Society found the average weekly salary of executive secretaries went from $109 to $184 or an increase of 68.8 percent; the average weekly salary for clerical employees went from $84 to $144.[4] The National Sec-

---

[4] *1975–1976 Office Salaries Directory*, Administrative Management Society, Willow Grove, Pennsylvania, p. 6.

retaries Association revealed in a 1975 survey of members—all of those who responded had at least five years of secretarial experience—that 60 percent earn annual salaries of $9,000 or more, while 28 percent earn $11,000 or more.

The salaries of administrators are also increasing. The Dartnell Corporation survey shows a jump of $52 per week in only one year.[5] In 1974, the business executive dictating to a secretary had an average weekly salary of $250; in 1975, that salary level increased to $302, and, in 1976, to $326 a week. Dartnell found that the average weekly salary for a secretary was $136 in 1974, $143 in 1975, and $159 in 1976.

Inflation also had an effect on the cost of stationery supplies in 1975, increasing them 20 percent; and fixed costs increased about 10 percent, due mostly to higher costs of heating fuel and electricity.

Improving secretarial utilization and increasing the productivity of executives are two major considerations in management attempts to bring office costs under control.

Saving time is of particular importance to people in management positions. As a person rises through the management ranks, more time should be spent on managing and less time on doing. Those in middle to top management positions should be spending from 50 to 70 percent of their time in thinking, planning, and improving interpersonal relations. In actual fact, many executives spend portions of the day just worrying about their lack of time. A typical middle manager or executive is fortunate to spend five percent of the day on planning. Fifteen percent is usually spent on the telephone, and another fifteen percent is spent at meetings. A large part of many an executive's time, over sixty percent, is spent on trivia, dealing with forms, reports, routine mail, and other tasks that should be delegated.

TRADITIONAL METHODS OF DICTATION AND TRANSCRIPTION

The traditional boss-to-secretary dictation method is only one of three possible methods for originating words. Alternative methods are writing drafts in longhand and dictating to a machine. Three possibilities also exist for transcribing dictation: by a secretary, by a typist, or through a specialized typing center.

Although the Bureau of Labor Statistics description indicates that a secretary must be able to take dictation at 110 words a minute and studies show that executives may dictate at rates up to 140 words a minute, it must be conceded that many executives do their planning of

---

[5] "Cost of Business Letter Rises to $3.79 for 1975," *The Secretary* (August/September 1975), p. 22.

dictation while the secretary is poised for dictation. The result is a waste of time while materials are organized for dictation. On the other hand, with machine dictation the word originator is forced to organize thoughts before the machine is activated.

Productivity is increased in typing situations, also, when work is centralized, routinized, and controlled. Long before modern word processing equipment was used, typing pools became an established method for handling large-scale production typing in offices. **Typing pools are simply centralized office areas set aside for production typing, where work is assigned to the typing staff under the close control of a typing supervisor.** Typing pools are the traditional training grounds for future secretaries, and "getting out of the pool" is considered a big step toward the goal of working for one boss. However, typing pools utilize electromechanical typewriters. The typist produces the finished work. In modern word processing, the finished work is no longer produced by the typist but by the machine. The typist becomes in effect an operator, monitoring the work of the machine.

COST OF OPERATION IN THE WORD PROCESSING SECRETARIAL MODE

Despite the cost of expensive word processing equipment, decreased labor costs give word processing the advantage over traditional modes of paperwork production. Costs are less when automatic equipment is used because fewer documents have to be retyped if a change is necessary. Also, word processing equipment eliminates the need for the multiple carbon copies that are the bugbear of both the executive secretary and the typist in the pool. The crucial problem in converting to a word processing system appears to be the need to fit the particular kind of work and quantity of documents produced to the proper kind of word processing equipment.

A realistic picture of word processing costs would have to include the overall saving in time and executive productivity as well as decreased labor costs resulting from the need for fewer secretaries than the traditional one-to-one executive-secretary relationship. A recent survey among 278 organizations indicates that 50 percent reported a decrease in secretarial staff resulting from the introduction of word processing. Of the 30 percent who reported no change, many indicated that more work was being turned out by the same number of secretaries. Among the 12 percent who reported increased staff size were comments indicating that the increase in secretarial staff was due to the increased volume of work from dictators.[6]

---

[6] *Word Processing and Employment*, New York: Deutsch, Shea & Evans, Inc., 1975, p. 3.

TRADITIONAL WORK HABITS AFFECTED BY WORD PROCESSING SYSTEMS

The most obvious change word processing brings to an organization is in the traditional one-to-one boss-secretary relationship. The word processing system deprives the office executive of an exclusive relationship with one secretary. Dictation equipment becomes the cold substitute for an interested, knowledgeable office assistant. Executives miss the support and loyalty provided by traditional secretaries. Sharing the services of an administrative secretary with several other executives is commonly perceived as a loss of prestige by managers and administrators. The traditional secretary, whose status is closely tied to that of the boss, also tends to view word processing as a threat to prestige. A survey of how word processing is accepted by people at various organizational levels indicates that although top management strongly favors word processing, upper middle managers, who tend to take the loss of status more seriously, are less strongly in favor. At every level, the secretarial staff is the most divided of all in the degree of acceptance.[7]

Support of top management is essential, therefore, if secretaries and executives are to make the required adjustments in work habits and procedures. In order to ensure the successful operation of word processing systems, many companies have had to implement executive training programs. Dictation training is often made mandatory for executives, to help them acquire proper methods for organizing their thoughts and for using dictation equipment. In standard practice few, if any, executives ever receive dictation training; yet the documents produced in word processing centers are only as good as the input by word originators. Since an efficient word processing system provides rapid turnaround (quick return of typed copy to the word originator)—usually from two to four hours—executives themselves soon discover the advantages in their increased productivity and a more efficient organization of work time. Another advantage of word processing systems is that the centralized dictation facilities usually operate 24 hours a day and can be used conveniently by phone from outside the office.

ADMINISTRATIVE SUPPORT FUNCTION IN WORD PROCESSING SYSTEMS

As studies of secretarial utilization show, approximately one quarter of a typical secretary's workday is spent taking dictation, typing, and proofreading. Three quarters of the time is spent on doing other things.

---

[7] Walter A. Kleinschrod, *Management's Guide to Word Processing*. Chicago: Dartnell, 1975, p. 30.

The other things frequently include tasks requiring lesser skills, such as reception, telephone answering, clerical posting, running errands, routine filing, and the like. When ambitious secretaries with special abilities are assigned work tasks below their capability, the result is secretarial boredom. Educated, intelligent secretaries want challenging, nonroutine work tasks.

In a word processing system, with the typing function reassigned to correspondence secretaries, the administrative secretary can be assistant to two or more managers, executives, or professionals. Such an assistant can free valuable executive time that is now spent on unnecessary administrative trivia. An administrative secretary normally receives work assignments from more than one executive or principal, and, in some offices, may handle work for three or more executives. Depending on the work load and office size, two or more administrative secretaries may work as a team servicing a group of executives. The basic administrative secretarial functions are opening and distributing mail, answering telephones and taking messages, and keeping an executive's private correspondence file. Additional functions and special projects can be added. Acting as an administrative assistant, the administrative secretary is capable of handling routine correspondence by dictating replies for an executive to the word processing center. If uncertain about a reply, the secretary can request a rough copy, have it edited by the executive, and then redictate it in finished form. The administrative secretary is capable of undertaking research, either statistical or factual, and drafting reports while working in close association with the executives involved. Travel reservations, scheduling of meetings, calendar- and record-keeping activities are other important duties executives can assign to an administrative secretary.

Operating as a member of the administrative support team provides the administrative secretary with excellent training in overall company policy, procedures, and organization, giving a broad knowledge and insight into the affairs of the company as well as an acquaintance with important company officials. Opening and reading the daily mail of several company executives familiarizes the administrative secretary with what is happening. By keeping copies of active correspondence in the administrative support area, the administrative secretary can respond intelligently in telephone conversations with principals and others. (See Figure 3-2.)

Depending on the office size, the team concept is most efficient when all administrative secretaries are located in one center or "hub" of operations, since one secretary is always there to cover the work station in case of absences or illness. The administrative support center should be located spatially near the principals served. (See Figure 3-3.) Whether a small satellite or a large company facility, the centralized administrative support center is the ultimate in the division of secretarial labor.

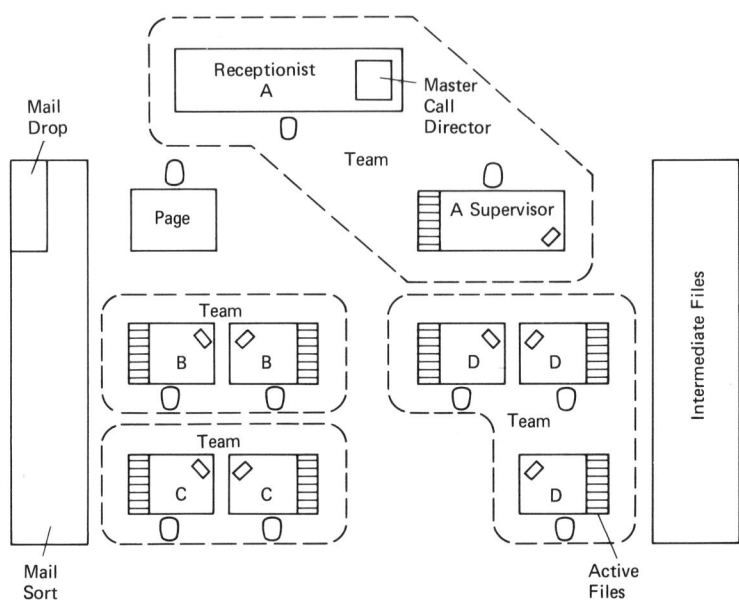

FIGURE 3-2 AN ADMINISTRATIVE SUPPORT CENTER

Detail of a hypothetical AS center, with aides divided into four teams. Team members fill in for one another, and can rotate to handle specialties assigned to other teams. Next to each AS aide's desk is active six-month file. Supervisor faces the secretaries; receptionist faces entrance to maintain control over incoming visitors and mail deliveries.

Source: Walter A. Kleinschrod, *Management's Guide to Word Processing*. Chicago: The Dartnell Corporation, 1975.

Administrative secretaries do little or no typing but work directly with word originators. In fact, they are word originators themselves, since they learn to dictate and edit the work of principals for redictating. Administrative secretarial training can provide an opportunity for members of the administrative support team to graduate eventually into mainstream corporate work in an executive capacity. Depending on the individual secretary and the policy of management, the job of administrative secretary can evolve naturally into that of an executive assistant to a top-level company official. Also, since professional secretarial supervisors are usually required to oversee the administrative support facilities, the position of administrative secretary provides another upward career opportunity into middle-level management as supervisor.

FIGURE 3-3 TWO ADMINISTRATIVE CENTERS

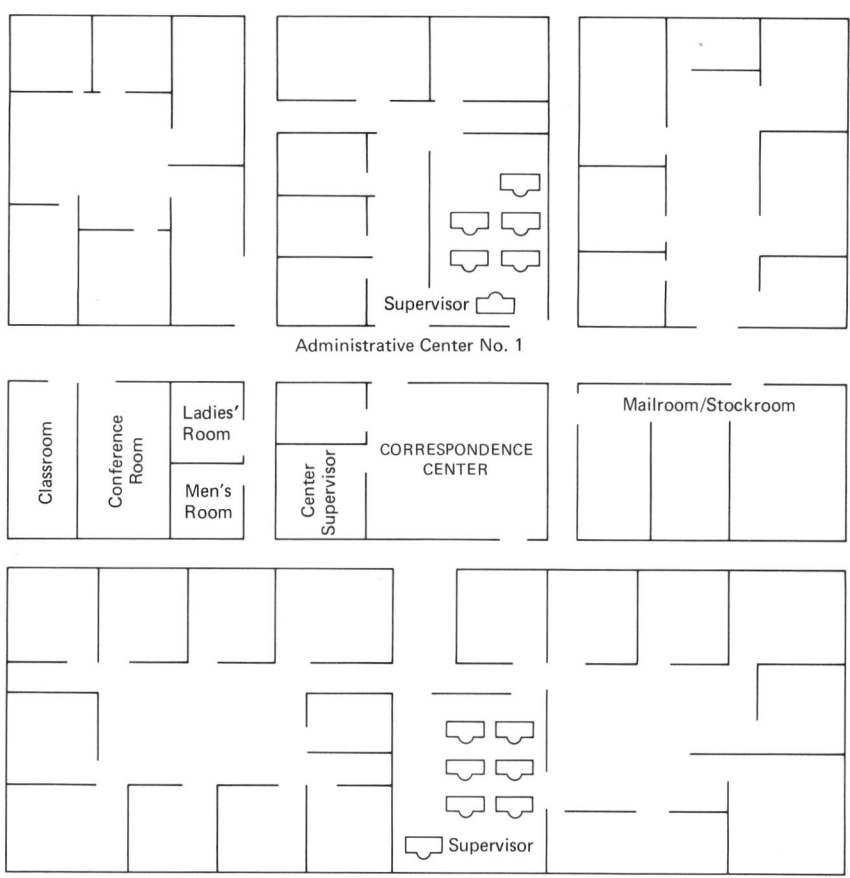

Two administrative centers, each serving half of the principals on the floor, flank correspondence center which handles typing for all the principals. This is only one of many variations possible in center placement within an office.

Source: Walter A. Kleinschrod, *Management's Guide to Word Processing*, Chicago: The Dartnell Corporation, 1975.

THE ADMINISTRATIVE ZONE—A COMPREHENSIVE WORD PROCESSING SYSTEM

Another more inclusive concept for a word processing/administrative support system is that of an administrative zone. As defined by one management consultant, an administrative zone is "a carefully planned grouping of logistic support services such as mail handling, stationery and supplies, photocopy work, typing, dictation services, filing, and records storage and retrieval, all located *within close proximity* to individuals requiring these services. Generally, the zone operates under the direction of a single supervisor." [8] The concept enables management to achieve two important goals—increased productivity and efficient administrative support.

Surveys by management have indicated that in many instances the private secretary's function is one of low productivity, high salary cost, and low levels of motivation and morale due to uneven work distribution and inadequate use of skills. The traditional use of typing and steno pools is not a satisfactory solution to these problems. In an administrative zone, however, the position of private secretary is replaced by the position of executive assistant, and new clerical and administrative positions become established to cover routine duties previously handled by secretaries.

Specialized personnel in the positions of central file clerks, photocopy operators, messengers, and general clerks perform efficiently, but at lower salary levels than secretaries, the routine tasks of filing, photocopying, in-house and out-of-house errands, coffee, and mail distribution. Typing specialists turn out finished documents of high quality and at high rates of productivity by working uninterruptedly; they also are capable of handling rush jobs and heavy, complex jobs in fast order. Centralized dictation equipment permits better distribution of transcription work. Administratively, a single supervisor in charge of an administrative zone ensures control over work distribution as well as increased productivity. For large-scale typing jobs, office executives funnel their requests through the supervisor, who can then organize the work staff to best advantage and assign appropriate numbers of typing technicians to meet deadlines as well as quality standards.[9]

The newly created position of executive assistant, which is essentially that of a senior administrative secretary discussed previously, can become an entry-level management position and thereby attract both male and female employees. An executive assistant provides support services for several executives, taking on special administrative assignments in order to relieve them of unnecessary detail work. The delegation of special projects makes the executive assistant a paraprofessional. The position can be a vehicle for growth, responsibility, and achievement on the part of an employee—motivators not always present in traditional secretarial positions.[10]

---

[8] Harold Tepper, "The Private Secretary: A Company Liability," *Management Review* (February 1973), p. 30.
[9] *Ibid.*, pp. 31–32.

The administrative zone arrangement provides management with the flexibility to assign clerical and secretarial staff efficiently and to absorb work in an economical and expeditious manner. By establishing linked, centrally controlled administrative zones throughout a large company, companies can benefit from uniform operating procedures, performance standards, and filing and retrieval systems. Standardizing operating procedures and filing systems in large organizations can result in significant savings in time and money. As filing and retrieval becomes increasingly automated, standards will necessarily require uniformity. In addition, administrative zones can be the source of career paths for clerical workers, offering different levels of responsibility, from file clerk to typing technician to executive assistant. The possibility of promotion provides employees with the incentive to get ahead and, in the process, reduces employee turnover—an added benefit to the company.[11]

FLEXIBILITY OF WORD PROCESSING SYSTEMS

The services of both the administrative secretary and the correspondence secretary are required in order to organize work flow effectively in an office word processing system. However, the system is highly flexible and can be adapted to the priorities set by management, whether those priorities are high productivity, quality, responsiveness, or executive convenience.

Originally it was planned by word processing equipment manufacturers that executive secretaries to top executives would be replaced by administrative secretaries and word processing secretaries. A recent survey by the Administrative Management Association indicates, however, that in some companies the executive secretaries to executives in the highest echelons are being retained although they send high-volume typing jobs to the word processing center. They are almost entirely outside the word processing system. Below the top executives the paperwork is practically all done in the word processing units.

The spatial arrangement of the typing and administrative support area can be as small as a two-person unit, one typing specialist and one administrative secretary. It can be expanded into a single large, centralized word processing center serving the needs of a large corporation, with several small administrative support work stations near the principals served. In a medium-sized company, perhaps a single combined administrative support/word processing center can handle all the secretarial support services for the company's executives.

In large law firms, where executive convenience and the ratio of one

---

[11] *Ibid.*

lawyer to one secretary are still common, a central word processing center producing a heavy volume of multipage legal documents may include correspondence secretaries, proofreaders, Telex and telecopier clerks, multilith operators, pages, messengers, and several supervisory personnel to ensure the high quality required in legal work. On the other hand, a large corporate office concerned with responsiveness of the word processing system to top management's needs may disperse small word processing/administrative support centers in each department or division, both to handle typing of letters, memoranda, and short reports, and to supply administrative support.

One major airline established a word processing system at its headquarters office near an airport. The system includes six separate locations. Two locations are administrative support stations and four are combined word processing/administrative support centers. The six units in the system, with a combined staff of 33 administrative secretaries and 16 correspondence secretaries, provide support to 304 word originators —a far cry from the one-to-one ratio of the traditional boss-secretary relationship.

In contrast, a small nonprofit organization with a total staff of 15 employees also uses a word processing system to organize work flow. The work of nine report writers and three administrators is handled by an administrative secretary (who is responsible for voluminous geographic files and mail), a word processing secretary (whose text-editing typewriter produces lengthy reports on economic conditions in third-world countries originated by the nine writers), and a receptionist/switchboard operator.

Configurations and combinations of word processing systems vary from company to company, just as the objectives of the organization, its staffing needs, and equipment needs vary. These variations only serve to emphasize the flexibility of the word processing concept and the ease with which word processing installations can be tailored to suit the needs of a particular organization. With this thought in mind, the next chapter will describe job titles and typical positions in a word processing system as well as some of the general personality attributes and characteristics best suited for the two distinctive positions of correspondence secretary and administrative secretary.

SUGGESTED READINGS

"Cost of Business Letter Rises to $3.79 for 1975," *The Secretary*, August/September 1975, p. 22.

Dartnell's Glossary of Word Processing Terms. Chicago: The Dartnell Corporation, 1975.

KLEINSCHROD, WALTER A. "The 'Gal Friday' Is a Typing Specialist Now," *Administrative Management*, June 1971, pp. 20–24, 27.

KLEINSCHROD, WALTER A. *Management's Guide to Word Processing*. Chicago: The Dartnell Corporation, 1975.

KONKEL, GILBERT J., and PHYLLIS J. PECK. "Traditional Secretarial Costs Compared to Word Processing," *The Office*, February 1976, pp. 66–67.

Occupational Outlook Handbook, 1976–1977 Edition. U.S. Department of Labor, Bureau of Labor Statistics, Bulletin 1875.

1975–1976 Office Salaries Directory, Administrative Management Society, Willow Grove, PA: 1975.

"The Office of the Future," *Business Week*, June 30, 1975, pp. 48–84.

TEPPER, HAROLD. "The Private Secretary: A Company Liability," *Management Review*, February 1973, pp. 23–42.

"Word Processing and Employment," A report compiled in cooperation with the International Word Processing Association by Deutsch, Shea & Evans, Inc., New York, 1975.

Chapter 4

WORD PROCESSING POSITIONS

The automation of secretarial work requires the separation of typing from nontyping tasks and, in the process, creates two new kinds of secretarial positions. The word processing or correspondence secretary is a typing technician; the administrative secretary is an assistant who works for more than one office executive. These two kinds of secretarial positions require different aptitudes and skills. Before considering the general range of position titles and job responsibilities that exist in a model word processing/administrative support system, let us examine the kind of personality and aptitudes best suited to these two different secretarial positions.

CHARACTERISTICS OF A WORD PROCESSING SECRETARY

In addition to fast, accurate typing skills, word processing or correspondence secretaries should have the ability—

—to be machine-oriented since a variety of complex equipment is involved.

—to comprehend quickly the capabilities of machines and use them to best advantage.

—to remain seated at a work station for extended periods while operating a machine.

—to concentrate despite noise and activities within the work center.

—to deal with quotas and to have work measured and closely scrutinized by a supervisor.

—to work under pressure of deadlines.

—to use common sense in thinking through and solving problems, such as typing what the originator means rather than what is dictated.

—to transcribe from handwritten or dictated material with a high level of efficiency.

—to handle small details and verify accuracy of typed text and to proofread for typing errors.

—to handle creatively the formatting of various kinds of documents, for example: letters, reports, lists, handbooks, brochures, manuals, speeches, newsletters, presentations, legal documents, financial statements, and others.

—to call on prerequisite verbal skills, including excellent vocabulary, spelling, grammar, and knowledge of punctuation rules.

—to understand teamwork and the need to coordinate work efforts with co-workers when faced with deadlines on heavy typing jobs.

CHARACTERISTICS OF AN ADMINISTRATIVE SECRETARY

Secretaries working in administrative support areas—areas that are, in theory, at the hub of office activity—require very different aptitudes and skills from those of word processing secretaries. The successful administrative secretary should—

—be people-oriented and enjoy working for several executives at one time.

—use tact and courtesy in the give and take of interpersonal relationships.

—be able to handle constant interruptions from telephones, executives, and co-workers.

—be able to concentrate on organization of tasks despite interruptions and distractions in a busy work area.

—be flexible in work habits.

—possess a good memory for people's names, dates, and events.

—have good vocal skills and telephone techniques.

—have good verbal skills for editing, proofreading, and initiating dictation.

—know shorthand, not as a prerequisite, but as a valuable extra skill.

—be resourceful enough to carry out independently special assignments that involve research and data collection.

—demonstrate to a principal various ways in which an administrative secretary's special capabilities can be used to the advantage of both.

—enjoy working as a team member in the administrative support area, filling in for absent co-workers and exchanging information.

The heart of any word processing/administrative support system is the human component. Without proper staff selection the system will not work. Not all people like to do the same things, and it is essential to fit the right person to the right job. By giving adequate consideration to the different characteristics required for the positions of word processing secretary and administrative secretary, personnel selection can be strengthened.

POSITION DESCRIPTIONS

The flexibility of word processing/administrative support systems is amply demonstrated by the number of ways in which organizations have adapted the concept to their own particular needs. Configurations are as varied as the companies using word processing. For the purpose of covering as many of the functions as possible, a model of a large, centralized word processing/administrative support system is shown in the diagram below. Typical job titles and position levels are given. These are followed by typical position descriptions for each title.

Starting at the entry level and proceeding to the top, the following are typical position descriptions for each job title, together with the qualifications required.

A MODEL WORD PROCESSING/ADMINISTRATIVE SUPPORT SYSTEM
TABLE OF ORGANIZATION

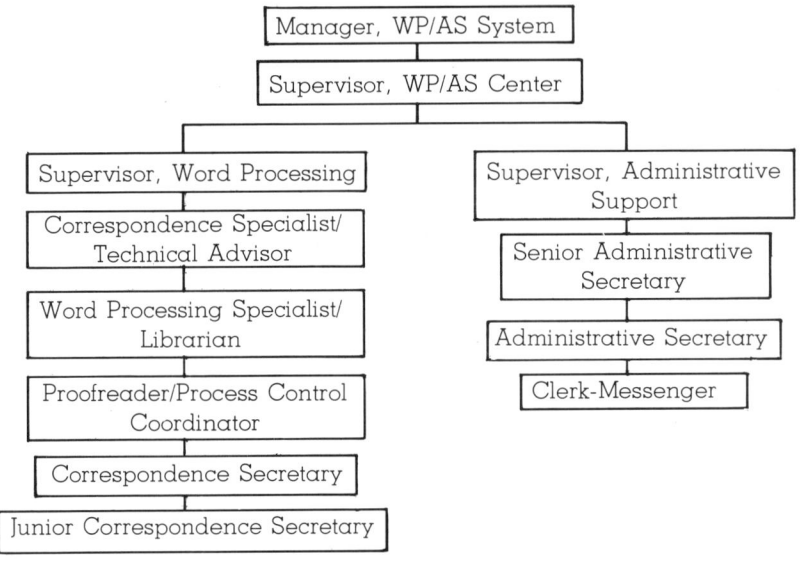

Word Processing

JUNIOR CORRESPONDENCE SECRETARY. Types material with average speed and skill from dictation media or from handwritten and typed copy on automated typing equipment, under close direct supervision. Good ability to utilize machine in correcting errors and making revisions. Efficient work organization and accurate recordkeeping of work performed. Works well with co-workers in the center. *Qualifications:* High school graduate. Type 45 to 50 words a minute accurately. Good knowledge of spelling, grammar, punctuation, and formatting. One year of secretarial experience preferred. On-the-job equipment training supplied.

CORRESPONDENCE SECRETARY. In addition to duties mentioned for the junior correspondence secretary, handles typewritten assignments of all kinds with accuracy and speed, under general supervision. Understands equipment capabilities. Has good knowledge of company terminology. Uses some discretion and judgment in carrying out work assignments. Cooperates with co-workers in sharing the work load. *Qualifications:* Types 60 words a minute accurately. Above-average knowledge of language usage. One to two years' experience as junior correspondence secretary in a word processing center.

Position Descriptions

PROOFREADER/PROCESS CONTROL COORDINATOR. Responsible for time and date stamping of incoming work, recording work in log, recording start and finish time. Maintains control sheets, records average lines per day, week, month. Proofreads transcribed material before it leaves the center. Handles confidential transcription. Periodically checks dictation equipment media. Handles telephone calls to and from departments and users. *Qualifications:* High school graduate, preferably with business school training or two-year college degree. Types 70 words a minute accurately. Excellent language skills and extensive knowledge of company vocabulary. Competence with a variety of complex machines. Three years' experience in word processing and thorough knowledge of company policy and procedures.

WORD PROCESSING SPECIALIST/LIBRARIAN. Performs highly complex operations using prerecorded material to set up complicated text and formats. Responsible for creation and maintenance of library of tapes containing recorded material. Requires little direct supervision and has thorough knowledge of all work applications. Responsible for own proofreading. Heavy statistical work. Assists in receiving, logging, and distributing incoming work, delegating and checking work of correspondence secretaries. Handles confidential transcription. *Qualifications:* High school graduate with business school or two-year college degree preferred. Types at least 70 words a minute accurately; statistical typing ability. Top language and formatting skills. Has complete knowledge of company vocabulary and company organization, policy, and procedures. Three to five years' experience in word processing or related secretarial work.

CORRESPONDENCE SPECIALIST/TECHNICAL ADVISOR. Technical expert on operation of all word processing machines in the center. Prepares tapes of complex formats for output by other secretaries. Prepares complex, multipage proposals and formats, financial statements, statistical reports. Problems of machine operation and procedures, as well as work simplification techniques, are prime concern. Provides technical guidance, training, and assistance to center personnel. *Qualifications:* High school graduate and specialized business training in two-year college program or on-the-job training. Types 70 to 80 words a minute accurately; has statistical typing ability. Top language and formatting skills. Complete knowledge of company vocabulary, policies, and procedures. Three to five years' experience in word processing or related administrative work. Knowledge of wide variety of word processing equipment.

SUPERVISOR, WORD PROCESSING. Interviews, selects new personnel, and evaluates performance. Responsible for work direction and training of staff. Establishes work procedures and controls. Ensures standards of performance for quality and quantity of output. Conducts periodic staff meetings. Ensures confidentiality of work when required. Resolves user problems with service. Maintains contact with management personnel. Designs and implements a management reporting system covering work measurement and standards. Plans annual budget for center, and new, improved secretarial services systems, with appropriate company officers. *Qualifications:* Four-year college degree or business school training and equivalent experience. Secretarial background and administrative experience. Thorough knowledge of word processing equipment. Proven managerial skills. Ability to delegate responsibility and to develop and evaluate personnel. Approximately five or more years' experience in directly related areas, including two to three years' in word processing.

Administrative Support

CLERK/MESSENGER. Handles nontyping clerical duties. Picks up and delivers work between departments served and the center. Keeps a check on supply inventory for the center. Reports to supervisor of the center. *Qualifications:* High school graduate. Dependable, willing to learn, ability to present courteous, helpful image to users of the center.

ADMINISTRATIVE SECRETARY. Provides administrative support for more than one principal. Handles mail, filing, telephone, and clerical duties. Little or no typing required. Qualified to compose and/or edit rough drafts of correspondence for principals and to dictate into the system. Responds to inquiries for routine information or material. *Qualifications:* High school graduate with additional college-level training or equivalent experience. Analytic ability and excellent vocal and verbal language skills. Ability to interact well with superiors, co-workers, and clients.

SENIOR ADMINISTRATIVE SECRETARY. Performs tasks of administrative secretary as well as administrative duties in handling of special projects and correlation of facts or figures. Fully aware of company policies and procedures. Makes arrangements for high-level company meetings and conferences, as well as travel arrangements for principals. May serve as assistant supervisor or group leader. *Qualifications:* Same as for administrative secretary, with approximately two years' experience.

SUPERVISOR, ADMINISTRATIVE SUPPORT CENTER. Possesses full mastery of administrative secretarial duties and, in addition, can handle difficult or confidential work for top management. Responsible for administrative support center operation. Selects personnel in cooperation with personnel department. Trains and evaluates performance of administrative support personnel. Establishes and maintains standards of quality in secretarial support. Specialist in work measurement. Prepares and controls budget allocations. Allocates the center costs to user departments. Resolves user problems. Maintains contacts with management, and seeks ways of improving and extending services to principals. Coordinates secretarial services with supervisor of word processing. *Qualifications:* Four-year college degree or equivalent work experience. Proven administrative secretarial skills. Thorough knowledge of company organization, policies, and procedures. Approximately five or more years of directly related word processing/administrative support systems experience.

SUPERVISOR, WORD PROCESSING/ADMINISTRATIVE SUPPORT CENTER. Directly responsible for operation of the center. Ensures maximum utilization of the center's personnel and equipment by coordinating and scheduling work. Determines staffing requirements, best uses of resources, need for overtime. Has overall responsibility for personnel development, training, and proper motivation. Serves as technical consultant in areas of systems and procedures, equipment and workflow. Has general knowledge of all facets of the center and understanding of overall goals. Evaluates the operation, develops new procedures, and maintains records. Participates in professional organizations to keep up with latest developments in the secretarial services field. *Qualifications:* Same as for supervisor of word processing or supervisor of administrative support. In addition, experience in work simplification is desirable.

MANAGER, WORD PROCESSING/ADMINISTRATIVE SUPPORT SYSTEM. Responsible for developing, planning, operation and control of multiple secretarial service units throughout the company. Develops long-range plans covering new and revised systems. Determines overall standards of performance, and ensures efficient procedures for handling and completion of paperwork and flow of information. Keeps management informed through adequate reporting process and controls on output. Determines format of reports, correlates complex data on workload statistics, and makes recommendations to management on projected budget figures for personnel and equipment. Provides orientation to new users of the word processing/administrative support system. Participates in professional organizations to maintain technical proficiency in word processing concept and equipment, and to keep abreast of latest developments in the secretarial services field. Usually reports to director of administration or vice president for administration. *Qualifications:* Four-year college degree or equivalent work experience. Proven managerial and administrative ability. Thorough knowledge of equipment, personnel, and work organization in word processing/administrative support centers. Knowledge of company policies and goals. Ability to interact effectively with middle and top management in achieving long-range goals of the organization.

WORD PROCESSING JOB TITLES

In a recent survey of 278 organizations using word processing, a total of 91 different job titles were found for people who operate word processing equipment.[1] The most frequently used title, "correspondence secretary," reveals no direct connection with word processing machines. The next two titles most frequently used, "word processing secretary" and "word processing operator," do indicate that connection.

The lack of standard job titles is a source of confusion to newcomers to the field and those seeking information or planning to enter the field. As an example, some of the more frequently used titles include:

correspondence secretary
word processing secretary
word processing operator/specialist/coordinator
word processor
operator (Mag Card, MC/ST, Vydec, Redactron, Wang, etc.)
typist or typing specialist
power typist
transcriber or transcription specialist
data/correspondence transcriber
technical clerk or machine clerk
communications or correspondence specialist
technician (word processing or correspondence)

The need for standardization of job titles is obvious. The Civil Service is presently working on the problem of classifying titles for government employees. However, from the private sector's point of view, standard word processing titles should not only describe the work but should also indicate that word processing jobs are attractive and different from other types of clerical work. If word processing is to attract newcomers to the field and also gain status within the corporate office for a special salary scale based on its unique merits, then standard job titles are a priority.[2]

---

[1] "Word Processing and Employment," a report conducted with the cooperation of the International Word Processing Association by Deutsch, Shea & Evans, Inc., New York, 1975, p. 11.

[2] *Ibid.*, p. 17.

Now that the various job titles and position descriptions for a typical word processing/administrative support system have been defined, the next chapter considers the effects that these staffing patterns have on actual people working in real office environments.

SUGGESTED READINGS

KLEINSCHROD, WALTER A. *Management's Guide to Word Processing*. Chicago: The Dartnell Corporation, 1975. Sections 4 and 12.

"Word Processing and Employment," a report conducted with the cooperation of the International Word Processing Association. New York: Deutsch, Shea & Evans, Inc., 1975.

Chapter 5

HUMAN ASPECTS OF WORD PROCESSING TECHNOLOGY

THE CHALLENGE OF THE 1970s

Like all human institutions, business institutions exist in a social environment; as the social environment changes, institutions, if they are to remain viable, must also change. A number of social and technological forces emerged in American society during the turbulent 1960s that provided a challenge to American business institutions. Some of these forces include: the continuing development of computer technology; increasing demands for equal opportunity and social justice for women, ethnic minorities, and the underemployed poor; changing social values and a desire for quality, not just quantity, in the American way of life; the shift from a production to a service economy, and the prospect that half the nation's workers will be in white-collar jobs by 1985; the growing influence of government in the affairs of individual Americans and business institutions.

FIGURE 5-1   SERVICE- AND GOODS-PRODUCING INDUSTRIES

Workers (in millions)

Service-Producing ——
 Transportation and
  Public Utilities
 Trade
 Finance, Insurance,
  and Real Estate
 Services
 Government

Goods-Producing ----
 Manufacturing
 Contract Construction
 Mining
 Agriculture

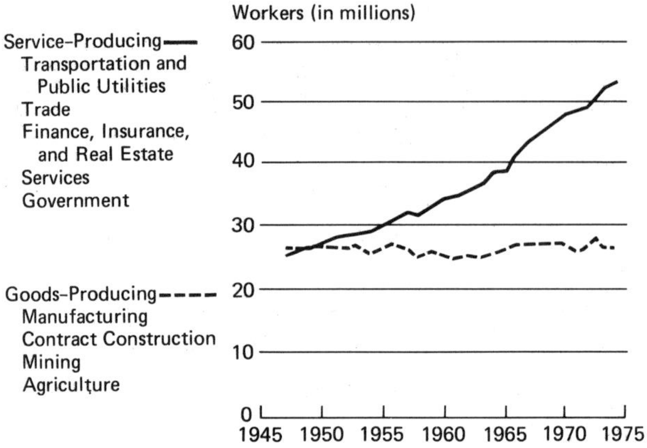

Source: Bureau of Labor Statistics.

In addition, there is a remarkable increase in the number of educated people in the work force; college enrollments in 1972 were up 38.2 percent over 1965. Educated workers seek jobs that are challenging and meaningful—jobs that offer the chance to learn and to grow. Statistics show that one in four American workers will have a college degree by 1985, although fewer than 20 percent of all jobs will actually require one.[1] All of these changes are factors contributing to the creation of a new social environment in today's business world.

Many business leaders are aware of the need for reassessing policies, procedures, and traditional human relationships in the office environment, if they are to attract and retain workers. Too often, however, business leaders attempt to use outdated values or management styles oriented toward the past, rather than recognizing the need for reorientation to the post-industrial era of the present. An industrial profile of the nation indicates that industries are either goods-producing or service-producing. As a result of automation and other technological developments, employment in goods-producing industries—agriculture, mining, construction, manufacturing—showed slower-than-average growth in 1974 over 1960. On the other hand, employment in service-producing industries—government, transportation, public utilities, wholesale and retail trade, finance, insurance, real estate, health services, education, and others—showed rapid growth in 1974, with about 19.8 million more workers than in 1960.[2] (See figure 5–1.)

---

[1] James O'Toole, "On-the-Job Learning," *Worklife* (January 1976), p. 4.

[2] *Occupational Outlook Handbook, 1976–77 Edition*, U.S. Department of Labor, Bureau of Labor Statistics, Bulletin 1875, p. 14.

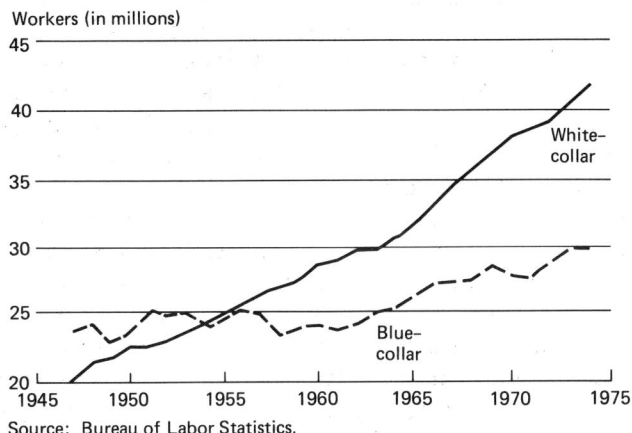
FIGURE 5-2 SHIFTS IN EMPLOYMENT—1945 TO 1975

Source: Bureau of Labor Statistics.

As a result, only about one third of the work force is engaged in the production of goods; most of the country's workers are currently in industries producing services. By 1974, blue-collar jobs held by craftworkers, operatives, and laborers were 12 million fewer than white-collar jobs held by professional, managerial, clerical, and sales workers.[3] (See Figure 5–2.) The difference between the industrial goods-producing era and the post-industrial service-producing era is not simply quantitative but is overwhelmingly qualitative, requiring a corresponding change in management technology.

The mechanical, industrial world of fragmentation, separation of operations, and interchangeable parts has been invaded by the instantaneous character of electricity. Automation in the electric era becomes a way of thinking just as much as a way of doing. Mechanical patterns of organizing each operation into a continuous sequence have been replaced by instant synchronization of numerous operations.[4] Electronic computers and word processing equipment provide typical examples of a new technology that has created totally new human environments. In our brief 200-year history as a nation, the socio-technological life-style of Americans has changed from that of the countryside, farming, the horse and carriage, railroads, and westward expansion, to that of cities, industry, the automobile, interstate highways, and space exploration. As a result of technological change, we live in a vastly different country than did nineteenth-century Americans, both socially and culturally.

A changing environmental system is an active process that produces

---

[3] *Ibid.*, p. 16.
[4] Marshall McLuhan, *Understanding Media*. New York: 1964, p. 349.

changes in the shape and scale of human relationships. The rugged individualism and laissez-faire opportunism typical of the age of mechanical industry are no longer the dominant aspirations of most Americans. Instead, wholeness, empathy, and depth of awareness become natural aspirations. "The mark of our time is its revulsion against imposed patterns. We are suddenly eager to have things and people declare their beings totally."[5] Integration and decentralization are the essence of automation technology.

In order to adjust to these changes, business organizations must place increasing emphasis on humanistic, democratic ideals and the quality of human life. Organization leaders must recognize that policies and procedures should take into account the human element, both within the organization and in the larger local and regional environment.[6] As socio-technical systems, business organizations have a responsibility to employees as well as to stockholders when planning future goals. More and more organizations are including in those goals not only the development of natural resources and capital goods but also the development of human resources.

A new science of man/machine/organization dynamics is needed, which places foremost consideration on the human element. Both machines and procedures used in a business technology must be related to the workers using that technology. Machines can no longer be misconstrued as having power over human beings. The long-held concept that machines are somehow responsible for turning workers into automatons is a myth. The machine is a product of human labor and ingenuity, created by human beings and easily altered by them. Human choice determines the way in which machines will be used. An automatic system of machinery opens up the possibility of doing away completely with unpleasant human work.[7] However, this possibility is thwarted when the work procedures implemented by management ignore the needs of workers and favor machine technology instead.

AUTOMATION AND
THE RATIONALIZATION OF WORK

The results of over a hundred studies during the past 20 years show that workers most want greater autonomy in carrying out their tasks and greater opportunity for learning and increasing their skills, as a means of achieving self-esteem and the esteem of others. Constant supervision

---

[5] *Ibid.*, p. 5.

[6] Gordon L. Lippitt, "Transition Management—Coping: Part 2," *Management World* (February 1975), p. 31.

[7] Harry Braverman, *Labor and Monopoly Capital.* New York: 1974, pp. 229–230.

and coercion, and monotonous and meaningless tasks are considered the two most oppressive and demeaning features of work.[8] These considerations hold true not only for autoworkers and steelworkers on factory assembly lines, but for growing numbers of white-collar workers. In fact, office automation in the production of typed documents bears a close resemblance to factory automation in the production of consumer goods. In both the office and the factory, machine technology is not the only factor involved in the process of automation.

The era of mechanical automation and mass production, introduced by Henry Ford in 1913, was based on two concepts—the subdivision of labor and interchangeable parts. Frederick W. Taylor's scientific management movement, which began over sixty years ago, follows the same logical concepts. Work is analyzed and broken down into separate operations that require a minimum of mental effort. In this way, human workers are reduced to interchangeable parts—eyes or hands—programmed to perform simple tasks. The intellectual component of work, on the other hand, becomes the prerogative of managers and supervisors, who exercise control over the rank and file of workers.

Mass production has given the American worker a high standard of living and many material benefits, as the proliferation of consumer goods and increasingly higher pay checks attest. However, the disadvantages inherent in dull, mindless work tasks tend to be expressed in terms of workers' resentment toward employers, sloppy work, and low productivity.[9] In recent years, growing numbers of plant managers are faced with major problems of absenteeism and high turnover due to the alienation of workers. The automobile industry and its assembly lines are a prime example of this situation; an illustration is the notorious strikes at the modern Lordstown, Ohio, plant of General Motors, where management determined work procedures on their own without consulting the workers themselves.

DATA PROCESSING AND THE DIVISION OF LABOR

The many similarities between data processing and word processing make experience with the human aspects of data processing useful in understanding recent trends in word processing. When the concepts of division of labor and interchangeable parts are applied to office work, as they have been in the data processing field, the result is a separation

---

[8] *Work in America*, Report of a Special Task Force to the Secretary of Health, Education, and Welfare. Cambridge, MA: 1973, p. 13.
[9] Lars E. Björk, "An Experiment in Work Satisfaction," *Scientific American* (March 1975), p. 17.

of intellectual from mechanical tasks. When electromechanical machines formerly used in accounting and plant inventory work are replaced by electronic computers, a further subdivision of work tasks occurs in the processing of data.[10]

Each level of the electronic data processing operation is now rigidly structured into a hierarchy of separate job titles and position descriptions, with different salary levels. At the management or intellectual level are the systems manager, systems analyst, and programmer. Below them at the clerical or operational level are the computer console operator, keypunch operator, tape librarian, and stockroom attendant. Entry into the highest level by a keypunch operator, for instance, who by hard work, additional training, and successive promotions reaches a top position, is highly unlikely. Instead, top-level jobs, where total knowledge and control of the computer system are lodged, are usually open to persons with appropriate college degrees and some prior top-level experience.[11]

The systems analyst is responsible for having a comprehensive knowledge of the data processed in the organization. With that knowledge, the systems analyst works out a machine system to cover processing requirements. Then the programmer converts the machine system into instructions for the computer. In the initial stages of electronic data processing, the programmer possessed much the same knowledge as the systems analyst. Now, however, the programmer position is becoming subdivided so that programmers at certain levels do not grasp the overall rationale for the system. Next, at the operational level, the computer operator feeds instructions to the computer through the console keyboard, following a rigid set of specified instructions that allow no deviation. At the bottom level of operations is the largest number of jobs created by computers—the keypunch operators. Since computers operate by processing information that is first carefully translated into uniform codes, keypunch operators prepare data for the computer by a mechanical punching of cards with the preassigned codes. Before the changeover to computers, keypunching operations were somewhat varied and occasionally required decisions on the part of the operator. Conversion to electronic data processing, however, has made keypunch work completely monotonous and repetitious. Large masses of data are usually presorted and prepared in ready-to-copy columnar format. Keypunch operators have thus become interchangeable pairs of hands and eyes transferring codes to cards.[12]

---

[10] Braverman, op. cit., p. 329.
[11] Ibid.
[12] Ibid., pp. 331–332.

WORD PROCESSING AND THE DIVISION OF LABOR

The division of secretarial labor, first introduced by word processing equipment manufacturers, led to the separation of traditional secretarial tasks into a technical/typing component and a human relations/nontyping component. Continuing trends in word processing indicate further subdivision of jobs.

At first glance, the specialized position of administrative secretary appears closer in responsibility to a management level of office work than the position of correspondence secretary, which is clearly situated at the operational level. The correspondence secretary's position is not unlike that of a computer console operator in data processing; whereas the administrative secretary, who may also be a word originator, has a position similar to that of a programmer, who works closely with the systems analyst and requires a broad knowledge of office policy and operations. Also, at first glance, the position of administrative secretary appears to resemble that of a traditional secretary minus only the typing function. These superficial similarities, however, require further examination.

Word processing systems have created two specialized secretarial positions, both of which have positive and negative human aspects. Consideration of both aspects will first be given to the role of administrative secretary, whose responsibilities are less clear-cut than the more obvious tasks of the correspondence secretary, whose role will be considered second.

THE ADMINISTRATIVE SUPPORT SIDE OF SECRETARIAL WORK

The position of administrative secretary lacks clear-cut lines of authority and responsibility. In theory, the administrative secretary, while working directly for two or more company executives, comes under the supervision of an administrative support supervisor. In actual practice, the administrative support supervisor usually comes into the picture only when conflicts arise, when peak work loads require additional secretarial assistance, or when a replacement is needed for an absent secretary. For the most part, the administrative secretary handles the routine telephone calls, filing, and mail distribution for the executives to whom he or she is assigned, as well as their special work projects. Salary increases or promotions depend on the recommendation of these executives. This divided authority is a potential source of friction.

Another possibly negative aspect of this job is that the taking of telephone messages and keeping of personal files can be assigned to lower-paid clerks. This is already happening in some companies. Such a subdivision of tasks leaves the administrative secretary responsible only for handling mail, drafting routine correspondence, and carrying out special projects. If employers' future cost-savings plans develop further, these services could conceivably be eliminated altogether or handled personally by each executive. Thus, in a series of gradual changes, the position of administrative secretary could be downgraded from that of an administrative assistant to clerical assistant, a position that requires a minimum of skill and rates a salary lower than that of a secretary.

However, a strong commitment by management to carry out affirmative-action programs in support of equal-employment-opportunity legislation, and to develop human resources within their organization can greatly strengthen the position of administrative secretary. The support of top management can ensure that meaningful work assignments will prepare administrative secretaries for possible careers in mainstream corporate work. One hopeful sign is in the number of companies currently implementing programs to achieve this goal. Some typical programs are discussed later in this chapter.

Another positive aspect of the administrative secretary's role is the tremendous advantage in working with several principals instead of only one. The administrative secretary can learn to handle a variety of duties and responsibilities, thereby acquiring a broad knowledge of company policies, organization, and operations. Human relations skills will be sharpened by a secretary who must juggle the priorities of several executives, keeping their appointment calendars, making their travel arrangements, organizing their conferences and business meetings, relaying their instructions to subordinates, and assuming increasing responsibility from their desks. In supplying support services, the administrative secretary must know how best to use office equipment in a cost-efficient manner. Many companies have programs for the cross-training of administrative and correspondence secretaries to supply them with an insight into the problems and pleasures of both sides of the secretarial coin. Knowledge of word processing equipment and of computer technology is vital to the administrative secretary, who will be working with computer printouts in support of company officers, and managerial and administrative principals.

In carrying out work assignments, the administrative secretary must also assume responsibility for her or his own career. Success in secretarial work is no longer dependent on one boss or one boss's advancement. Working for several executives gives the administrative secretary an opportunity to prove that she or he can take on added responsibility by identifying innovative ways of assisting without infringing on the principals' job responsibilities. Unlike the traditional secretary, who supports one executive's career goals, the administrative secretary shares with several executives a common purpose and works along with them as a valued team member to achieve corporate goals.

CAREER PATHS FOR ADMINISTRATIVE SECRETARIES

Between 1969 and 1974, when the supply of college graduates rose 8 percent, the number of women with four-year college degrees going into secretarial work increased by 100 percent. New job openings for educated workers, predicated on rapid economic growth, have become increasingly scarce; in fact, the 12.9 percent of the work force in the manager category in 1948, had grown by less than 1 percent in 1973.[13] Ambitious graduates who plan to use secretarial work as a stepping-stone to management level positions, however, should not become completely discouraged. In making a commitment to the word processing concept, a number of companies are also making a commitment to provide career paths that reflect the abilities and goals of secretarial employees.

One approach to the problem, taken by Standard Oil of Indiana and the National Broadcasting Company, is to designate each secretarial employee either as a "professional secretary," who finds secretarial work rewarding in itself, or as a "progressional secretary," who seeks upward mobility into management. Thereafter, progressional secretaries aspiring to work in areas other than word processing, are considered for positions that will integrate them into the corporate staff in line with their background and training.[14]

A formal developmental approach is contained in a paraprofessional program implemented by PepsiCo International, where the administrative secretary in the word processing system is actively involved in the special projects, programs, and functions of the department. PepsiCo inaugurated a word processing system in 1974, and the staff now includes 28 administrative secretaries and 12 correspondence secretaries to support 108 principals. Some 80 percent of the principals are technical or professional staff. Paraprofessional jobs are viewed by PepsiCo personnel as intermediate positions between top-level professionals and lower-level secretaries. The most likely area for the development of openings for upward mobility has been in administrative services.

Three word processing supervisors periodically evaluate the secretar-

---

[13] O'Toole, op. cit., p. 4.
[14] "Building a Paraprofessional Structure into WP," *Administrative Management* (September 1974), 67.

ial work originating in each department at PepsiCo. If the work becomes heavy or specialized enough, there may be a possibility of creating a new administrator or coordinator—a position into which a secretary can move as a paraprofessional. Among former administrative secretaries who have moved up after receiving paraprofessional training is a budget coordinator in the marketing department, an assistant traffic coordinator, and a personnel administrator. A former correspondence secretary took company-financed college courses in data processing and programming and is now a document assistant/librarian in the systems area. The program is one example of a planned effort to give secretaries a chance for advancement and the necessary training to succeed.

Specialized in-house training programs and outside tuition-paid college courses are being recognized by an increasing number of employers as a long-range investment and a means of developing their employees more fully. The IBM Corporation, for instance, has 275 education centers within the company and encourages employees to assess their own needs and to develop themselves and their careers by using these centers. Xerox Corporation supports its own International Center for Training and Management Development, which represents a $75-million investment and features new and unusual educational techniques. Kimberly-Clark has a program encouraging employees to take up to one year of educational leave with pay for work-related study as well as two weeks of annual leave with pay to attend school. Career-minded secretaries in word processing, who hope to branch out into other areas of work, will find increasing opportunities for achieving their objectives through on-the-job training programs. In the future, "learning a living" may become possible for employees of more and more business institutions.[15]

THE WORD PROCESSING SIDE OF SECRETARIAL WORK

The word processing or typing side of secretarial work bears a close resemblance to the work of a computer console operator. The operator transmits instructions to the computer through the terminal keyboard, which is actually a typewriter keyboard with some additional keys. In like manner, a correspondence secretary types coded instructions and text at draft speed into the automatic typewriter or CRT-microcomputer word processing system. There is no need to type the material in finished form as a typist would on a standard typewriter. (As a result, a correspondence secretary eventually loses this particular kind of typing skill.) Instead, the machine transforms the drafted material into finished

---

[15] O'Toole, op. cit., pp. 5–6.

form, following the coded instructions of the secretary. The correspondence secretary is in fact a machine operator, and the finished work or output is a product of the machine, not of the human typist. The output of the machine is beyond any human skill in both quality and quantity.

In the process of operating word processing machines, the correspondence secretary utilizes specialized language, proofreading, and formatting skills, as well as skill in manipulating the machine to best advantage. However, personal contact with office executives and other word originators can become infrequent or nonexistent. The word processing supervisor usually acts as a mediator between the word processing staff and those outside the center. Thus, the social skills required in traditional secretarial positions tend to be under-utilized in word processing.

Recent emphasis in the field has been on the establishment of standards to evaluate word processing systems, measure the output of equipment, and improve the performance of operators. The creation of production standards is simply a step in applying scientific management principles to typewritten output. If a word processing supervisor knows that an average correspondence secretary doing a form letter job plays out 300 envelopes in 50 minutes, then a standard of 6 envelopes per minute can be established. The work of all correspondence secretaries can then be compared with this standard. If they do not measure up, extra training on the machine or, if there is still no improvement, replacement of the secretary may be the solution. Standards are also a means of evaluating operators for raises and promotions. The primary importance of standards, however, is in the control they give to supervisors and management over production and work scheduling. In peak work periods, knowledge of the time it takes to perform a particular job makes it possible for a word processing supervisor to schedule and distribute bits and pieces of work recorded on a number of magnetic tapes or disks. Correspondence secretaries then automatically transcribe meaningless words completely out of text of whole documents. In a job that is already considered "high-pressure," the introduction of standards and tight controls adds to the pressures on people working in word processing centers.

THE MECHANIZATION OF OFFICE WORK

The sociologist, C. Wright Mills, writing some twenty-five years ago, describes the mechanization of work:

> In its early stages, a new division of labor may specialize men in such a way as to increase their levels of skill; but later, especially when whole operations are split and mechanized, such division develops certain faculties at the expense of others and narrows all of them. And as it comes more fully under mechanization and centralized management, it levels men off

again as automatons. Then there are a few specialists and a mass of automatons; both integrated by the authority which makes them interdependent and keeps each in his own routine. Thus, in the division of labor, the open development and free exercise of skills are managed and closed.[16]

In today's electronic era, the young field of data processing continues to develop a division of labor in accordance with Mills' analysis. As in factory work, measurement of output, emphasis on speed, and supervisory controls in office work are the logical accompaniments to the simplification and mechanization of work tasks. The result can be the industrialization of clerical work, and, as is happening in data processing, the office atmosphere can closely resemble that of a factory. Complete knowledge of the work process is limited to a few management people, and each worker at succeeding lower levels of the office hierarchy handles a specialized segment of the process at decreasing levels of pay. Jobs at the lowest level, that is keypunch operators, involve the simplest, most mechanized segments of the whole process and are the lowest paid. Not only is there little chance of advancement, but the more work is rationalized from the top, the faster the jobs at the lowest level tend to increase.[17]

Although still in its infancy, the evolving field of word processing seems to be following data processing down the same archaic path, applying organizational concepts of a bygone era to today's office environment. It is evident that word processing's popularity with top management is based on cost savings and increased productivity, which means fewer high-salaried employees producing more work.

Some companies are applying outmoded work procedures to the new technology, so that word processing centers are simply regarded as the same old typing pools equipped with expensive new machinery. Correspondence secretaries are seen as doing the drudge work of the secretary's job, the implication being that not much intelligence is needed to type. The staff in word processing centers in these companies tends to form into close-knit groups, so that a split develops. One group tends to feel that work is dumped on it by the other group, a situation that creates friction and low morale.

EMPLOYEE MORALE
IN WORD PROCESSING CENTERS

Problems typical of industrial mass production are also becoming typical of word processing centers—absenteeism, job dissatisfaction, and high turnover of personnel. Training of typing specialists in word processing centers is costly, and, therefore, employers are concerned to

---

[16] C. Wright Mills, *White Collar*. New York: 1951, pp. 227.
[17] Braverman, *op. cit.*, pp. 335–336.

> ### Satisfaction Scales Used in MSQ
>
> Intrinsic
>
> 1. ability utilization
> 2. achievement
> 3. activity
> 4. advancement
> 5. compensation
> 6. co-workers
> 7. creativity
> 8. independence
> 9. moral values
> 10. social service
> 11. social status
> 12. working conditions
>
> Extrinsic
>
> 1. authority
> 2. company policies and practices
> 3. recognition
> 4. responsibility
> 5. security
> 6. variety
>
> The MSQ uses a five-point rating scale and respondents are asked to rate each item according to how they feel about the item on their present job: 1—Very dissatisfied; 2—Dissatisfied; 3—Neither dissatisfied nor satisfied; 4—Satisfied; 5—Very satisfied. The scores for each type of job satisfaction are obtained by summing the ratings assigned by the respondents to the appropriate dimensions.

FIGURE 5-3

find ways of improving the situation. A study of correspondence secretaries working in word processing centers, mainly in the Minneapolis-St. Paul metropolitan area, selected one secretary at random from each of 74 companies participating. The study attempts to measure job satisfaction of the 74 magnetic typewriter specialists. A short form of the Minnesota Satisfaction Questionnaire, shown in Figures 5-3 and 5-4, was used.[18]

---

[18] Mona J. Casady, "Job Satisfaction of Typewriting Specialists in Word Processing," *Words* (June 1974), pp. 3–5.

Job Dimensions and Descriptive Statements

(General or Overall Satisfaction)

1. **Ability Utilization** — The chance to do something that makes use of my abilities.
2. **Achievement** — The feeling of accomplishment I get from the job.
3. **Activity** — Being able to keep busy all the time.
4. **Advancement** — The chance for advancement on this job.
5. **Authority** — The chance to tell other people what to do.
6. **Company Policies and Practices** — The way company policies are put into practice.
7. **Compensation** — My pay and the amount of work I do.
8. **Co-workers** — The way my co-workers get along with each other.
9. **Creativity** — The chance to try my own methods of doing the job.
10. **Independence** — The chance to work alone on the job.
11. **Moral Values** — Being able to do things that don't go against my conscience.
12. **Recognition** — The praise I get for doing a good job.
13. **Responsibility** — The freedom to use my own judgment.
14. **Social Service** — The chance to do things for other people.
16. **Social Status** — The chance to be "somebody" in the community.
17. **Supervision, Human Relations** — The way my boss handles his men.
18. **Supervision, Technical** — The competence of my supervisor.
19. **Variety** — The chance to do different things from time to time.
20. **Working Conditions** — The working conditions.

FIGURE 5-4

The results showed that compensation and amount of work performed together with their relations with co-workers were of most satisfaction, and advancement and social service or opportunities to do things for others were of least satisfaction to the 74 magnetic typewriter operators in the study. Three satisfaction scales were used in the test—the characteristics of the job (intrinsic scale), the characteristics surrounding the job (extrinsic scale), and job dimensions and descriptive statements (general or overall satisfaction scale). In a comparison with 227 office clerks who took the same test, the 74 correspondence secretaries scored lower on each of the three satisfaction scales. Statistically, the differences proved to be significant for both the intrinsic and the general or overall satisfaction scales. (A significant difference is one that cannot be due to chance.) No significant difference was found between the two groups in the extrinsic scale.

Another recent study of a word processing center at Wright Patterson Air Force Base, with a staff of nine clerk-typists in job classification GS–4 or GS–5, also indicates job satisfaction and motivation as significant problem areas. Employee absenteeism and requests for reassignment made clear the need for the study. The motivating potential scores of IBM Mag Card Typewriter operators averaged 23.5, and Mag Card II operators averaged 19.6 in the word processing center. Comparison of these scores with a study of government clerical workers who averaged a score of 124 on the same test amply demonstrated the need for a more effectively designed job.

The recommended solution was to give the word processing clerk-typists maximum independence and flexibility to schedule their own work, determine the appropriate procedures, and select the equipment in the center that was most appropriate for the job. In addition, the word processing supervisor's job description was revised to reflect the *loss* of routine scheduling, control, and work checking tasks that had been given to the clerks. Results of the study show that when given the necessary latitude, the word processing clerk-typists became highly motivated to grow and solve increasingly difficult job problems on their own.

In effect, the results of the Air Force study and the recommended solution are very similar to those of a two-year experiment in work satisfaction made among 12 assembly-line workers in a machine plant in Sweden. The decision-making body for the experiment consisted of representatives from management, the unions, and the workers, together with three researchers—an industrial engineer, a psychologist, and a social psychologist. Preliminary analysis by the researchers indicated that the social system in the unit under study ". . . had become 'hung up' on the technological system in ways that contributed neither to fulfilling the unit's objectives nor to the workers' satisfaction."[19] A major change suggested initially by almost all the workers in the unit was to eliminate the conveyor-belt assembly line and use a large table instead. This arrangement permitted freer, less monotonous work activity. During the course of the experiment, workers found that the belt was a useful tool when they controlled its speed; eventually elements of the belt were reintroduced in the work area.[20]

As the experiment progressed, new social relations developed among the 12 workers in the unit. Each man learned to carry out the entire sequence of operations, and gradually teams formed to handle all as-

---

[19] Björk, op. cit., p. 19.
[20] *Ibid.*

pects of production. Group cooperation replaced the former one-man, one-machine organization; the workers coordinated their efforts and assumed responsibility for the unit's work objectives and for one another.[21]

In evaluating the project, one observes a quantifiable change in productivity—an increase of about 5 percent. More important, however, is the increase in learning that is also evident, and its consequences for long-term productivity. The men now share common goals and are knowledgeable about the flow of materials and production schedules. Rush orders and changes in delivery dates are no problem, because the entire operation is flexible. Although work satisfaction is difficult to measure, an obvious sign of increased satisfaction is the fact that none of the 12 workers wants to return to the old system. In examining the process of change that took place in the unit during the two years of the experiment, the researchers found confirmation that people are capable of controlling their own work situation and, at the same time, of getting out from under the domination that production technology places on them and their social status. The experiment gives reason to think that delegation of autonomy to the worker may eventually replace the bureaucratic autocracy, characteristic of the workplace in most Western nations, with an egalitarian democracy.[22]

PEOPLE-ORIENTED WORD PROCESSING

Now, while still in its infancy, the word processing field represents a challenge to business administrators and managers to prove that the sophisticated technology of word processing equipment can be matched by an equally sophisticated technology of democratic policies and work procedures governing its use. The right combination cannot help but result in satisfied employees who enjoy their work, and whose productivity will produce an efficient, profitable operation. Many professionals in the word processing field are aware of the challenge and are attempting to emphasize the notion that people are the heart of any word processing operation.

A pioneer in the development of word processing, Reg Little, supervises a centralized word processing system at Air Canada headquarters. Mr. Little notes that the most common fault in potential word processing managers is in spending too much time in evaluating equipment and not enough in considering people.[23] One suggestion he gives for a successful word processing operation is the proper training and motivating of staff. A basic assumption is the overwhelming need for

---

[21] *Ibid.*, p. 21.
[22] *Ibid.*, p. 23.
[23] Reg Little, "Considering People," *Words* (Autumn 1975), pp. 25–27.

selecting the proper people. (See personal characteristics of word processing secretaries in Chapter 4.) Adequate and proper instructions to staff include *what* to do, *why* to do it, *how* to do it, and *when* to do it. New employees are thoroughly briefed on the word processing center's rules of operation, line-count measurement and the reasons why they must measure their work (to charge it back to the departments using the center), details of the office equipment, telephone answering, photocopy and stationery procedures, turnaround standards, and the like. In effect, each employee is given an overall view of how the total system operates in the center, and the reasons behind policy and procedures.

Instead of standardizing text-editing equipment, Air Canada uses several kinds of keyboards for different applications. CRT units are used for heavy editing work; magnetic tape typewriters are used for general correspondence, reports, and phototypesetting; built-in memory typewriters are used for short documents that will not be retained. The word processing staff thus have an opportunity to learn the operation of a variety of text-editing units and work on a variety of documents. This learning possibility has proven a strong motivational factor among the staff even though it introduces some training and scheduling problems for the supervisors.[24]

Quality of work is considered equally important as quantity at Air Canada's word processing center, and employee training emphasizes that productivity without quality is meaningless. Quality in work standards in turn produces workers who are likely to take pride in their work. Mr. Little believes that work in a word processing center can become dull unless employees are told how well they are performing. Each month, employees make a confidential summary of their performance for the word processing center supervisor. After that, the monthly productivity figures for the center are given to the employees, with the highest average productivity and error rate, which they can compare with their own productivity and error rate. In this way, measurement statistics are not used as a whip but as a means for each individual to evaluate her or his own performance. In the process, they learn how their efforts contribute to the total group effort. This type of feedback provides an incentive for each person to pull his or her own weight.[25]

According to Dr. Lane Riland, director of psychological research and services at Eastman Kodak, people involved in an organizational change, particularly as drastic a change as word processing, must feel that they have some control over the situation and be given a real understanding of the proposed change, the reasons behind it, and the expected benefits. Participating in and planning the change can de-

---

[24] *Ibid.*
[25] *Ibid.*

velop a different set of attitudes and feelings. Participation frequently results in commitment. Therefore, executives, secretaries, and administrative support personnel should all be involved in the planning and organization of the word processing center.[26]

Typing technicians in the center are too often isolated from the people who originate the work, and word originators too often feel the center is off-limits. Executives should be encouraged to visit the center when possible and get to know the typing specialists who handle their work. A periodic "open house" or other suitable type of social gathering should be scheduled for this purpose. If an executive has a serious complaint, it should be taken up with the supervisor, but compliments for a job well done should be delivered in person by the executive to the word processing staff member. An executive dictating into a telephone in a central dictation system should keep in mind that another person—not an automaton—will eventually transcribe the dictation. Inserting a bit of humor or informality into the proceeding will help both persons involved to reassert human domination over the mechanical apparatus.[27]

Another facet of people-oriented word processing is the interesting possibility that the position of secretary may be about to lose its exclusive connotation as women's work. Men are gradually entering the word processing field, attracted by the complex machines and the opportunity for independence in completing work tasks. Once men start competing with women for jobs in word processing systems and the sexual division of labor in secretarial work is eliminated, secretaries in general may enjoy increased respect and prestige.

THE CHALLENGE OF AUTOMATION TECHNOLOGY

Many word processing supervisors are former secretaries with many years of administrative experience. Word processing offers these persons a chance for advancement, and many of them have become the strongest proponents of word processing. They see in word processing attractive career opportunities based on the example of a few pioneers in the field who have already attained management jobs. However, the emphasis on advancement and upward mobility in word processing may be somewhat premature. Many of the earliest word processing centers were organized along the same lines as the typing pools they replaced. Although large word processing centers continue to be hierar-

---

[26] "Successfully Planning The 'Human Side' of Word Processing," *Administrative Management* (October 1973), pp. 39–40.

[27] Bert Vorchheimer, "Cleaning Up the Office Dump," *Management World* (July 1975), pp. 26–32.

chical in structure and provide supervisory positions, the trend in word processing appears to be toward small centers with less formal structures. Emphasis on technical proficiency and creative use of the equipment itself may provide longer-range job satisfaction than emphasis on career paths. Professionals in all fields find intrinsic satisfaction in their work and in their personal development, not in upward mobility alone.

The word processing center is a communications network with a technology capable of processing knowledge at incredible speed. Word processing secretaries are technicians and imaginative professionals, capable of handling work assignments on their own initiative or in collaboration with word originators; close supervision is not needed. A team leader rather than a supervisor is appropriate for a professional word processing staff, a leader selected informally by team members to handle the function of work coordination when necessary, and to act on occasion as intermediary with personnel and management representatives.

The real challenge in word processing at its present stage of development is the equipment itself. Although automatic machines operate in a specialized way, they are not limited to one particular kind of work. Instead, the logic in word processing machines incorporates a power of adaptation that purely mechanical typewriters lacked. As anything becomes more complex, it becomes less specialized. Human beings are the least specialized and most adaptable of the species on earth because of the complexity of the human brain and central nervous system.

Although word processing equipment is still in its earliest phase, the diversity and range of its applications are amply demonstrated by the typical case studies described next in Chapter 6. The complexities of the various kinds of automated machines provide the possibility of a continuing on-the-job learning experience in the word processing field, a challenge that should intrigue typing specialists for some years to come.

SUGGESTED READINGS

BJÖRK, LARS E. "An Experiment in Work Satisfaction," *Scientific American*, Vol. 232, No. 3, March 1975, pp. 17–23.

BRAVERMAN, HARRY. *Labor and Monopoly Capital*. New York: Monthly Review Press, 1974.

"Building a Paraprofessional Structure into WP," *Administrative Management*, September 1974, pp. 66–68.

CASADY, MONA J. "Job Satisfaction of Typewriting Specialists in Word Processing," *Words*, Vol. 3, No. 2, June 1974, pp. 2–5.

LIPPITT, GORDON L. "Transition Management—Coping: Part 2," *Management World*, February 1975, pp. 28–32.

LITTLE REG. "Considering People," *Words*, Vol. 4, No. 3, Autumn 1975, pp. 25–27.

McLUHAN, MARSHALL. *Understanding Media*. New York: McGraw-Hill Book Company, 1964.

MILLS, C. WRIGHT. *White Collar*. New York: Oxford University Press, 1953.

O'TOOLE, JAMES. "On-the-Job Learning," *Worklife*, January 1976, pp. 2–6.

Special Task Force to the Secretary of Health, Education, and Welfare. *Work in America*. Cambridge: The MIT Press, 1973.

"Successfully Planning The 'Human Side' of Word Processing," *Administrative Management*, October 1973, pp. 39–40, 42, 44.

VORCHHEIMER, BERT. "Cleaning Up the Office Dump," *Management World*, July 1975, pp. 26–32.

Chapter

WORD PROCESSING CASE STUDIES

The following case studies range from a word processing center in one location with a staff of three correspondence secretaries to an organization with offices located across the country, having a total word processing staff of over one hundred persons linked together by a network of communicating magnetic card typewriters. Banks, an insurance company, a hospital, a hotel, a management consulting firm, a national food company, the subsidiaries of an oil company and a chemical company, a utility, a law firm, and a government agency are included in the studies. A broad range of equipment is used and analyzed.

Some of the studies cover a period of several years and indicate changes in equipment and procedures that evolved as a result of increasingly higher workloads. Many of the case studies demonstrate that new and better applications of word processing equipment have been evolving over time. In line with the evolutionary scheme, case studies are presented on an equipment continuum, ranging from the simple to the complex. They start with stand-alone automatic typewriters and progress to communicating typewriters, CRT video display microcomputer word processors, and finally to computer word processing systems. In the process, the automated machines become increasingly sophisticated and operating the machines becomes increasingly uncomplicated as more and more "skills" are built into the machines themselves.

Case Study
No. 1 Kansas City, Missouri

Crown Center Hotel[1]

BACKGROUND. In a consumer-oriented market, hotels must satisfy their guests in order to operate at a profit. Hotel department heads traditionally need the services of a private secretary, since most hotels operate as large conglomerates made up of numerous departments. The Crown Center Hotel in Kansas City, a Western International Hotel, has 13 departments. They include the executive office, accounting, sales, catering, food and beverage, repair and maintenance, housekeeping, laundry and valet, recreation, front office, and security. As a means of coordinating all departmental functions into a single, efficient operation, while at the same time reducing the cost of providing secretarial support, the management of the Crown Center installed a word processing center in 1972.

STAFF AND EQUIPMENT. The word processing center has three secretaries, who work under the general supervision of the managing director's secretary. Equipment consists of three IBM Executive Mag Card typewriters, three telephone dictation recorders, and three transcribers. If one recording machine is busy, the call is automatically transferred to the next open recorder. Dictation time is at a 20-minute limit during night hours and at 10 minutes during the day, and the recorders operate 24 hours a day. The dictation equipment has the capability not only to record dictation but also to revise any section of the dictated material. The center is used by approximately 48 people, including the various department heads.

---

[1] "Word Processing Environment at Crown Center Hotel," *The Secretary* (October 1973).

PROCEDURES. Most of the work of the word processing center comes in over the telephone. Everything is done first in rough draft. Executives are asked to dictate letters exactly as they want to see them in the finished version, indicating date, address, number of paragraphs, enclosures, and number of carbon copies required. A review course is held periodically to refresh the word originators' memories on the transcribing process, which differs from the traditional boss-secretary situation, and to remind the department heads of the cost factors involved in using the center.

The catering department takes bookings over the phone, and the word processing center provides the clerical backup for this operation. In fact, the catering department provides 50 percent of the center's work. Secretaries in the word processing center are familiar with on-going activities in each of the other departments of the hotel also, since they are in constant contact with them. The first step in recording dictation is that the person dictating identify herself or himself. The word processing secretary is then mentally prepared for the subject about to be transcribed. With the hotel area identified, the secretary can think ahead to the best way of handling the work. Once work is completed, the secretary delivers it in person to the respective manager. This procedure helps to personalize the operation and broaden the secretary's knowledge of different areas in the hotel.

Each communications secretary receives a manual describing work responsibilities and priorities, letter composition and format. An on-going periodic evaluation process of each secretary's work consists of a review session held every six months with the supervisor. Criticisms and appraisals are discussed, and secretaries are encouraged to express their views.

PRODUCTIVITY. The hotel management finds that the word processing center has many advantages. Centralizing all correspondence and other typewritten material in one area gives managers better control over production. The cross-training involved when three secretaries transcribe for all the various hotel areas eliminates delay in getting the work out if someone is ill or on vacation. When two secretaries transcribe dictation, recording it simultaneously on mag cards, the mag cards are given to the third secretary for playout, thus getting more than 30 percent increased production. This is an efficient way of catching up after a busy weekend of recording.

The savings in office equipment, floor space, and salaries for three secretaries (rather than thirteen) are self-evident. After four years of operation, results justified management's initial decision. The typewritten product is much better, not only in quantity but also in quality.

Case Study
No. 2 Springfield, Illinois

Illinois National Bank of Springfield[2]

BACKGROUND. The Illinois National Bank of Springfield moved into a new five-story building in 1975 and installed a new word processing center. In the same year, the bank opened a new off-premise banking facility with a staff of thirty people, a new customer service department with a staff of five, and increased the teller line by four. Bank assets increased by more than 10 percent to a total of $186 million. Total staff has held constant at 268, however, due to increased administrative efficiency and normal attrition. Prior to centralization, some twelve secretaries worked full-time on typing tasks, and twenty clerk-typists typed about half the time. Typing is now centralized in the word processing center, and former typists are working as administrative assistants.

STAFF AND EQUIPMENT. The word processing center is directed by a word processing supervisor with a staff of five correspondence secretaries. Equipment includes six IBM Mag Card II typewriters and six IBM 6:5 cartridge dictation systems with Touch-tone telephone input. The center operates 24 hours a day for dictation. It serves about eighty word originators in the bank's main office and off-premise facility. The strong backing of top management and a policy that makes the use of the center mandatory are important factors in the success of the center's operations. Strict enforcement of the rule has paid off in increased efficiency. However, some eighteen typewriters are still in use within the bank, primarily for incidental typing tasks.

PROCEDURES. Letters, farm and real estate appraisals, trust and financial reports are the kinds of typed documents turned out by the center. Standard correspondence of about 500 different types, such as customer savings and greeting letters or meeting notices, are recorded on mag cards. Variable data, such as names and addresses, are put on a second card. The Mag Card II automatically plays out the information on the two cards by a process called "switch coding," to produce personalized error-free letters. Prompt, personal communications produced by the word processing center help project the bank to customers as a responsive, friendly institution.

---

[2] Jeffrey D. O'Neal, "We Increased Typing Productivity 340%," *The Office* (February 1976), pp. 95–96, 98, 100.

PRODUCTIVITY. The center's five correspondence secretaries do the work formerly handled by twenty-two secretaries and typists. Typing productivity has increased 340 percent and turnaround time decreased by 75 percent. Regular correspondence is completed in two hours maximum, compared with the previous one day or more. A significant reduction in the cost of supplies has resulted from decreased need to retype documents because of errors. Some 2,000 to 2,500 documents are turned out monthly, amounting to approximately 40,000 to 50,000 lines a week.

Case Study
No. 3   Stamford, Connecticut

State National Bank of Connecticut[3]

BACKGROUND. State National Bank of Connecticut has its executive office in Stamford and its largest branch office in Greenwich; in addition, the bank has offices in three counties of southwestern Connecticut. In all, there are 43 locations. The work of some departments of the bank does not involve correspondence or any form of written material. However, in 1969, the bank's executives decided to establish a word processing center in the Stamford office because the paperwork was increasing rapidly. Some secretaries were frequently overloaded with work while others were on vacation. The word processing center was planned to service all the bank's branches and departments over a considerable distance, some as far as 50 miles away. This was made possible by the bank's courier system, which requires couriers to make regularly scheduled runs calling on each branch of the bank seven times during a working day.

STAFF AND EQUIPMENT. From two typists serving personnel in the Stamford and Greenwich areas in 1969, the center has grown to five correspondence secretaries and a word processing supervisor. The center is located in Bridgeport. Equipment includes one Redactron and four Wang dual-tape automated text-editing typewriters and four Dictaphone System 193 Thought Tank recorders with a word controller console. All bank personnel have access to the center for dictation; approximately seventy people use it on a regular basis. All confidential material is handled by the supervisor of the center.

---

[3] Priscilla Tunkel, "Central Dictation System Triples Typing Output Over Four-Year Period," *Corporate Systems* (October 1975).

PROCEDURES. Form letters and certain types of documents are stored on tapes and coded. When a user wants a particular document or letter, specific instructions to the center include the code number along with any changes or deletions. Secretaries of bank executives, especially, use the dictation system for coded form letters to avoid repetitive typing and thus increase their own productivity. When a secretary is busy or away on vacation, a bank vice president relies on the center for secretarial support. One bank officer, who spends a lot of time visiting different branch offices and calling on bank customers, simply telephones memos and letters to the center at the end of each day. Upon returning to his own office the next day, the correspondence is typed and ready for signature.

PRODUCTIVITY. Delivery of typed documents turned out by the word processing center is handled by the bank's couriers. On low priority material, those bank locations farthest from the Bridgeport center receive a two- to three-day turnaround time. Work received from locations closest to Bridgeport is completed in one to two days; high priority work is done the same day. In its first full year of operation, the word processing center produced 121,792 lines. Four years later the figure was 359,033 lines. As more branches and departments start to use the center and learn its advantages, the upward trend is expected to continue.

Case Study
No. 4 Montclair, New Jersey

Mountainside Hospital[4]

BACKGROUND. The word processing center at Mountainside Hospital keeps the laboratory and pathology departments, as well as the hospital's School of Medical Technology, running smoothly. The school and the two departments are innovative in the use of word processing equipment. Three pathologists and four pathology residents keep 15 dictation units at their workbenches, in their offices, and in the morgue. Pathologists must use both hands while cutting and measuring specimens and focusing microscopes. Therefore, microphones are conveniently mounted on the benches to pick up their voices as they dictate their findings. One pathologist mounted a microphone directly on his microscope. The units are activated by means of foot pedals.

---

[4] Jeanne A. Kraemer, "Mountainside Hospital's Inventive Approach," *Word Processing* (July/August 1975).

STAFF AND EQUIPMENT. Five full-time secretaries operate four IBM Mag Card Selectric typewriters and one Mag Card II machine. The center operates up to ten hours a day, seven days a week.

PROCEDURES. Pathology reports are more or less standard, and the dozen or so most-used reports are prerecorded on magnetic cards. In dictating, the pathologists simply specify the measurements of the particular specimen and the particular report form to be used. Transcription is now a matter of a few seconds rather than the time previously required to type out entire reports.

Autopsy reports formerly required a production cycle of some three days, but with magnetic cards, the process has been reduced to about four hours. In producing the pathology and autopsy reports, accuracy is essential for both medical and legal reasons. Each draft formerly had to be proofread by pathologists. The new procedure frees them from this largely clerical task. Rather than reading the entire document each time, only the insertions, corrections, and revisions have to be read when turned out on the Mag Card typewriters.

When a new lab test was introduced at the hospital before forms for it were designed and printed, the Mag Card II was used to supply forms automatically by running off up to 500 every week. Time cards for laboratory personnel are also run off on the Mag Card II. In addition, the meeting minutes for three different hospital committees are stored on magnetic cards, as are form letters, procedural changes, memos, employment correspondence, and personnel forms.

PRODUCTIVITY. A typical month's work in the word processing center consists of about 1,600 pathology reports, a dozen lengthy autopsy reports, a flood of laboratory forms, procedure manuals, course outlines, lectures, and research papers, as well as the usual load of correspondence.

Case Study
No. 5 San Francisco, California

Del Monte Corporation[5]

BACKGROUND. One of the largest and best known food companies in the world, Del Monte receives a constant flood of letters from customers, consumers, students, and the general public. Company policy is to

---

[5] "Del Monte Packs Quality in Word Processing," *Infosystems* (June 1974).

reply to each in a highly individual manner, and centralized transcription was in effect for some fifteen years at Del Monte. At one point, the pool involved over twenty secretary-typists. Services were inadequate, however, and as departments hired secretaries in an attempt to handle the work, the central pool dwindled to three typists. As a result of increasing payroll for secretarial services, management turned to automated techniques of word processing.

STAFF AND EQUIPMENT. Two supervisors and four secretaries (three for input and one for output) service seven departments and some eighty active word originators. Transcription secretaries type on Magnetic Tape Selectric typewriters. One secretary operates two Magnetic Tape Selectric Composer units for playback. Input to the center is through an IBM Word Processing System in which desk telephones (dial input stations) are connected to the word processing center. Word originators dial a designated number on their desk phones, which connect to one of five input recorders in the center. By dialing 5, the originator can contact the supervisor in the center. The system has built-in safeguards against one person listening in on or altering the dictation of another person in any way.

PROCEDURES. Dictation is handled on a first-come basis unless a job is designated *rush*. Dictation is recorded on magnetic belts and an entire belt is transcribed in rough draft at one time. Since the company requires a double check for accuracy, the rough drafts are proofread by a supervisor as well as by the transcription secretary. After proofing, the magnetic tapes are mounted onto two Magnetic Tape Selectric Composer systems. The text is then played back, on appropriate letterheads for the various departments served by the center, at the rate of 150 words a minute. One secretary can operate the two automatic machines simultaneously. Composer systems produce finished copy, proportionately spaced in print-like quality. Finished letters are delivered to word originators by a messenger-clerk who makes pickups and deliveries every half hour.

A consistent company image and policy is made possible by using standard format and product terminology in correspondence regardless of the department that originates the letter. Letters cover a range of topics, from products, supplies, and quality assurance from the marketing division, to shipments and claims from the traffic department. The center also maintains magnetic tapes that store pesticide schedules, a telephone directory, distribution center inventory lists, traffic rate cards, and price lists. These are updated and reproduced in standard format periodically.

PRODUCTIVITY. The center prepares over 400 original documents a week from dictation and another 200–250 repetitive, prerecorded letters. Most letters are one-page, from 17 to 24 lines in length. Routine correspondence is returned to the originator in four hours or less, and rush jobs in 90 minutes. By installing a word processing system, Del Monte has reduced administrative costs by $100,000 a year.

Case Study
No. 6   Dallas, Texas

Natural Resources Group of W. R Grace & Company[6]

BACKGROUND. The headquarters of W. R. Grace & Company is in New York City, but the Natural Resources Group moved to Dallas to be closer to its major operations. The group's operations in paper, petroleum, mining, and energy services are located in the west and south. The group has coal mining interests in Colorado, Kentucky, and West Virginia, and produces oil and gas from U.S. fields as well as operations in Canada and Libya. Contract drilling, refined product storage, and terminaling in the U.S. are other company activities, as is supplying service and equipment to oil and gas wells in the U.S. and Canada. Monthly operating reports, sent to New York from Dallas, contain a wealth of statistical data as well as some 150 to 200 pages of text. Tables of statistics can range from 10 columns to 500, and pages must be fanfolded. Larger statistical compilations measure up to 11 inches deep by 10 feet wide.

STAFF AND EQUIPMENT. The Dallas word processing center has a manager and a staff of 14 to operate the 14 Xerox 800 dual-tape electronic typing system stations. Each tape cartridge used with the machine holds up to 66,000 characters, including formatting instructions. The center also has four Lanier Tel-Edisette recorders, each taking 12 tape cassettes, for use by group executives for regular dictation and by field personnel in transmitting memos and reports for transcription and distribution. The headquarters staff numbers about 105.

PROCEDURES. The monthly operating report is due in the New York headquarters of W. R. Grace & Company on the third Tuesday morning of each month. Usually it is transported aboard an early morning plane

---

[6] "A W. R. Grace & Co. Word Processing Center," *The Office* (February 1976).

from Dallas. As a rule, the report is prepared in not more than four or five working days, and last-minute changes require extensive revisions. As the information for the operating report comes in to the center, largely in the form of handwritten text and tables, a workflow coordinator assigns it to one of the 14 typing technicians. They use 8½-inch continuous-form paper for the text and 14-inch continuous-form paper for the tables. The pages are later cut and duplicated in a uniform 8½ by 11-inch size, using a reduction duplicator for oversize pages. In addition to the monthly operating report, the center also handles weekly divisional field reports, extensive correspondence, memos, and other communications.

PRODUCTIVITY. The monthly operating report is the biggest single job handled by the center. Distribution requires thirty-seven complete sets of the voluminous report, plus a number of partial sets for various divisions and sections of the company. About 80 percent of the center's work is statistical. When only 12 typing technicians are operating, output has ranged from 35,000 to 50,000 lines during weeks when the monthly operating report was not part of the work.

Case Study
No. 7 New York, New York

Teachers Insurance and Annuity Association and College Retirement Equities Fund[7]

BACKGROUND. A Manhattan-based nonprofit insurance company, TIAA-CREF is an outgrowth of the Carnegie Foundation for the Advancement of Teaching. Colleges, universities, and other educational institutions are served by the two organizations in the areas of retirement annuities, life insurance, and medical plans. Among the 1,800 or more legal reserve life insurance companies in the U.S., TIAA-CREF ranks fourteenth in total assets. In 1975, TIAA-CREF had some 400,000 participants and 2,947 institutions providing one or more TIAA benefit plans for groups of staff members. The company has no agents or branch offices, and all of its documents and correspondence originate in the New York office.

A transcription department with a staff of four typists and a supervisor was set up in 1963 to handle letters dictated by correspondents in four departments of the company. The staff had grown to 17 by 1973, and equipment included 15 IBM Magnetic Tape Selectric typewriters and a

---

[7] Dolores T. Marinelli, "Matching the Industry Gait," *Word Processing* (July/August 1975).

FIGURE 6-1
Supervisor Dolores Marinelli and the attractive, spacious word processing center at TIAA-CREF.

remote dictation system. (See Figure 6–1.) Frequently used material was stored on magnetic tape, and precoded instruction sheets were used by word originators to designate material the secretary was to pick up from tape for a completed document, and where changes (if any) were to be made in the stored material. However, communication and understanding between the secretaries and the word originators was lacking. The secretaries in the center were classified and paid as typists, and turnover was high. Although the center produced a large volume of work, quality and efficiency needed improving.

STAFF AND EQUIPMENT. After a streamlining of work procedures and job classifications, the word processing center now includes 18 magnetic card units—12 Mag Card IIs and 6 Mag Card Selectric typewriters—and 6 IBM Tone Input System recorders to handle dictation from more than 100 word originators. A staff of eight word processing specialists, one senior word processing specialist, seven correspondence secretaries, one correspondence assistant, and one trainee provide secretarial support to over 400 people at the New York headquarters.

PROCEDURES. The new Mag Card II typewriters required the conversion of model precoded paragraphs from 350 magnetic tapes to more than 6,000 magnetic cards. Each card contains one paragraph, coded and filed according to the user department. The 6,000-paragraph library is the core of the center's operation and provides prerecorded material for most of the documents originated by user departments—Policy Service, Premium Administration, Underwriting, and Individual Counseling. Anywhere from 10 to 20 ground leases are prepared annually by the Investment Law division, each of which contains more than 100 pages. The center turns out the leases in substantially less time than the full week it formerly took one secretary.

A long-standing procedure allowed only the supervisor in the center to resolve a dictation problem directly with a word originator. To help break down the communication gap between secretaries and word originators, the procedure was altered: now secretaries phone the person directly to clear up problems in the dictation. By creating a professional environment and career advancement for secretaries within the center, the turnover problem resolved itself. The staff in the center now takes pride in turning out work of superior quality. An informal education program in word processing is maintained by the supervisor of secretarial services, who collects and circulates to the staff newspaper clippings, magazine articles, and new books relating to the dynamic field of word processing.

PRODUCTIVITY. Transcription turnaround time in the center ranges from 15 minutes to four hours. Death claims must be handled within 24 hours, so turnaround time is critical. The center has an outstanding accuracy rate, with less than 1 percent of all work returned for correction. The record was achieved during a year in which 220,000 pages of type were produced and the conversion was made to the magnetic card library.

**Case Study
No. 8   Redding, California**

CH2M Hill[8]

BACKGROUND. CH2M Hill is a management consulting firm, created by a merger of Clair A. Hill & Associates with Cornell, Howland, Hayes & Merryfield. It has offices located across the country, from Virginia to Oregon. Although top management executives at the firm always de-

---

[8] Bette Primrose, "Coordinated WP Yields Big Savings and High Morale," *Administrative Management* (November 1975).

pended on a centralized typing center rather than on private secretaries, the concept of word processing was introduced in 1972. Typing centers were then upgraded into an integrated, coordinated system. Complete standardization of equipment, procedures, format, and paper was applied throughout the company, and a firm-wide word processing coordinator was appointed. Typists in the word processing centers were given the new title of "word processor." They were provided with a standards manual, now used by all offices of the company, covering punctuation, capitalization, abbreviations, margins, and other elements of style. The result is substantial savings and improved quality. For example, an engineer in Anchorage, Alaska, preparing a report, can have a page added by a consultant in Redding and still maintain stylistic consistency and author control before the final report is transmitted to Corvallis, Oregon, for printing.

Communicating Mag Card typewriters in word processing centers and the IBM 1130 computer in the Redding office make it possible to improve communications over long distances. If a project is handled by a team of experts from different disciplines at various locations, their work can be pulled together and compiled at the single work station most convenient to the project. In addition, if the workload becomes too heavy at that station, another distant word processing station can lend a hand without any difficulty.

STAFF AND EQUIPMENT. The company employs a word processing work force of 100 or more. Word processing centers are equipped with and use the same magnetic cards either on IBM Executive Mag Card Selectric typewriters or on Mag Card IIs. The change in title from "typist" to "word processor" has improved morale and encouraged word processors to keep improving and do more. Word processors in the Redding office learned the commands and language needed to input a large specifications document into the IBM 1130 computer. Now both computer output text and automatic typing output are routine assignments for people in the Redding word processing center.

Because of standard operating procedures and the Communicating Mag Card, setting up a word processing system in a new office is a team effort. When the Sacramento office opened, the initial heavy workload was shared by other locations. Everyone knew what to do, thanks to the standardized formats and guidelines.

PROCEDURES. The word processing coordinator for the system receives a weekly departmental summary of machine utilization from the supervisor in each word processing center. The summary records the number of pages done by each word processor on each machine. When work measurement shows that the use of the machine does not justify the cost, the equipment is removed, since the hardware is covered by lease agreements. The reporting system also allows supervisors to monitor the quantity of work turned out by each word processor. Knowing the amount of work each station is expected to do permits the budgeting of personnel accordingly.

An annual seminar attended by all word processing supervisors in the company is a means for exchanging ideas, improving the system, and developing goals for the coming year. Many ideas come out of these seminars that help in solving problems of low morale, employee turnover, quality control, turnaround time, and workload scheduling. The seminars also reinforce a sense of pride in team effort as well as individual growth and recognition among the secretarial force.

PRODUCTIVITY. Improved communications between word processing supervisors uncovered the fact that word processing centers in five offices had not been charging clients for work done. After correcting this error, some $26,000 additional revenue was generated. Standardization permits purchasing supplies in volume for the word processing centers and, in the first year alone, resulted in a saving of $30,000. Another $5,000 was saved by switching from rental to leasing agreements for the Mag Card equipment and other hardware. In the first full year of operations, secretarial productivity increased by 30 percent, and the company saved over $85,000.

Case Study
No. 9   Houston, Texas

Chevron Oil Company Geophysical Division[9]

BACKGROUND. Chevron-Geophysical, a wholly owned subsidiary of Standard Oil Company of California, serves as an exploration processing center for the worldwide operations of its parent company. Word processing is highly technical and ranges from short letters and memos to lengthy reports, manuals, program documentation, and textbooks. Reports dealing with scientific formulas and mathematical equations require the typing of many superscripts, subscripts, and Greek symbols. Changing fonts or print wheels by hand delays the work. Most of the work received in the word processing center is handwritten, heavily revised, and haphazardously put together. Since technical authors rarely have clearly legible handwriting, much of the transcription involves guesswork and frequent corrections. Some 67.3 percent of the work is revised.

---

[9] Nina R. Everhart, "Technical Word Processing at Chevron-Geophysical Div.," *The Office* (February 1976).

Word Processing Case Studies

In 1969, six secretaries with electric typewriters and one dual-tape automatic typewriter were trying to handle the workload at the Houston headquarters, where personnel had increased from 22 to over 300. A work study by management showed the need either for three additional secretaries or the installation of four more single-tape automatic typewriters for the six secretaries in the center. The single-tape machines were installed in 1970; but, by the end of 1972, the center's equipment configuration had changed to two single-tape and four dual-tape automatic typewriters. In 1974, the workload was expected to double (in fact it tripled); and, after searching and testing various kinds of equipment, management installed CRT minicomputer machines.

STAFF AND EQUIPMENT. The word processing center presently has five word processing secretaries handling work for more than 200 principals. Equipment includes four off-line minicomputer machines with CRT video screens, two typewriters with a memory storage capacity of approximately 200,000 characters each, and a Telex machine. An electric typewriter is used for envelopes, mailing labels, and so on. Every secretary is capable of operating all the equipment in the center. In addition to handwritten work, input is by means of a centralized dictation system, as well as by portable dictation equipment. A sixth word processing secretary with an automatic typewriter in a remote location handles work for the president and three other executives in top management, as well as confidential work for other principals.

PROCEDURES. Each word processing secretary is assigned to a group of principals. This allows the secretary to become familiar with the work of each word originator and to set priorities. If workflow is heavy or problems arise, they call for assistance from co-workers. Secretaries are responsible for the quality of work output and for assisting others when their own workflow is slow. The fact that everyone knows all the equipment makes for excellent teamwork. Moving from one machine to another during an emergency is a simple matter. Staff members take pride in their work; and the center is a source of pride to the company, as well. The high morale of the word processing center staff is shown by an average job tenure of twelve years.

PRODUCTIVITY. The technical nature of the work demands a training period of six months before a secretary achieves good production standards. Standards are high; and, with the installation of the CRT minicomputers, production soared. From an overall average of 14 pages per day on the tape units, word processing secretaries went to 47 pages per day on the minicomputers. Turnaround time varies with the length of document, equations, and handwriting legibility, but, on letters and memos, finished work is turned out the same day.

Case Study
No. 10 Washington, D. C.

Congressional Research Service of the Library of Congress[10]

BACKGROUND. A department of the Library of Congress, the Congressional Research Service (CRS) prepares reports on subjects dealing with legislation and other Congressional business for the members and committees of the U.S. Senate and House of Representatives. Requests may be for analytical, historical, background, or factual data. The CRS is divided into eight divisions, each with a staff of research specialists who prepare reports in the fields of American law, economics, education and public welfare, environmental policy, foreign affairs, government and general research, and science policy. The eighth unit is the senior specialist division, which covers a variety of areas.

Reports range in length from one to 600 pages. In 1973 the CRS received 200,000 requests for reports. At least 40 percent of these requests required original research, which means that each report was typed and revised at least once. Researchers prepare the reports, which are then typed by a support clerical staff. The clerical staff, using electric typewriters, was unable to keep up with the material developed by the research staff in response to increasing numbers of requests from Congress. In addition, reports are often needed immediately to provide background for current legislation and Congressional hearings.

The CRS management undertook a review of the processes and methods used to prepare and type the research reports. Sophisticated electronic equipment seemed to provide a solution to the steadily mounting workload. A thorough search and review was conducted to determine the scope and capabilities of word processing equipment and its possible applications to the needs of the CRS.

PROCEDURES AND PRODUCTIVITY. Traditional units of measure for typewritten production—words and lines per page—are not valid in the CRS material because of quotations, footnotes, and bibliographical data that appear frequently in the research reports. Therefore, in assessing the output of the word processors assigned to each of the eight research divisions, the standard of individual keystrokes was considered the most valid unit of measurement.

Each research division includes a small typing staff. An on-the-job test of three systems, representing units with magnetic tape, magnetic

---

[10] "Library of Congress Steps into Word Processing," *Government Executive* (July 1975).

	Production Time For 1000 Keystrokes	Average Operator Training Time	Cost For Five Working Days (Including Rental Supplies)	Cost of Operation per 1000 Keystrokes
Electric Typewriter Magnetic Tape Cassette Unit	21.0 minutes	32 hours	$ 57.10	$20.38
Electric Typewriter Magnetic Card Unit	10.4 minutes	32 hours	$ 85.04	$14.92
CRT and Proportional Spacing Typewriter Magnetic Tape Cassette Unit	6.1 minutes	6 hours	$113.17	$11.56

cards, and cathode ray tube (CRT) with tape cassette was undertaken for 90 days under actual operating conditions. The test commenced with the introduction of the three different systems into the normal routine and workflow of the foreign affairs, American law, and science policy divisions of the CRS. The processed reports were of varying length, format, and language difficulty. CRS clerical staff, trained by the manufacturers of each system, kept detailed logs. Final tabulations were made, gauging the keystrokes-per-hour productivity of all final work.

Operators were also asked about the difficulty of learning and operating the equipment, improvements they could suggest, and their general attitudes toward the equipment. Other staff members in the same vicinity were questioned about noise and other environmental distractions caused by the equipment. The test results shown in the chart above provided the CRS with the necessary figures to determine that the CRT system was the most effective equipment for their needs.

Each report prepared by the word processing units of the CRS is not only turned out in typewritten form for the members of Congress and their staffs, but it is also fed electronically into a computerized data bank. In the future, more and more reports will be generated from the data bank, eliminating the need for searching through voluminous paper files or for retyping.[11]

---

[11] "Washington Innovates to Cope with Paperwork," *Business Week* (June 30, 1975).

STAFF AND EQUIPMENT. Seventeen CRT units were installed in the CRS research divisions, with one magnetic tape unit retained by the Library Services Division for automatic letter writing, bibliographic lists, and other miscellaneous functions. The CRT units were operational and productive one week after installation. Untrained operators learned to work the CRT units by watching and working with other trained operators on the staff. No formal training was necessary. The video system was the most readily acceptable by CRS management, clerical staff, and researchers because of the high-quality output, increased speed, ease to learn and operate, and relative quiet.

Case Study
No. 11   New Haven, Connecticut

Bergman & Barth [12]

BACKGROUND. The firm of Bergman & Barth is one of New Haven's larger law firms, with a staff of 12 lawyers. The firm's practice is restricted to federal, state, and foreign taxation; estate planning and probate; pensions, corporate financing, and profit sharing. In recent years, the relaxation of regulations governing professional corporations and the increased supervision of pension and profit-sharing plans by the Internal Revenue Service has resulted in a considerable increase in the volume of paperwork. The firm's involvement in real-estate syndications has contributed to this increase. Three secretaries with three magnetic tape typewriters and a considerable storage of **boiler plate** (model documents) failed to meet the firm's requirements. Standard repetitive text filled 160 magnetic tape cartridges, but few variations were possible without increasing the typing workload and proofreading time. A real-estate syndication, including the partnership agreement and offering statement, can total 140 pages in length. Revisions and corrections were being made directly to the appropriate pages, and the secretaries were expected to replace these pages in the draft. However, no complete original of the document was left for reference, and errors in the draft substitutions were always a possibility. When increasing workload made the services of a fourth secretary and a fourth magnetic tape typewriter a likely prospect, the firm decided to seek an alternate and better solution.

STAFF AND EQUIPMENT. After some consideration, an LCS Compu-Text word processing system, built around a minicomputer, was installed. The system includes magnetic disk storage, four typewriter termi-

---

[12] David L. Reynolds, "An In-House Word Processing System," *Law Office Economics and Management* (Fall 1975).

nals, one video typing station, and a line printer. (See Chapter 7 for further details and photograph.) One of the typewriter stations, referred to as a **dedicated slave typewriter**, is used for output only. Each of the three magnetic disks in the system can store up to 1,500 pages of copy. Two disks are dedicated to client business, and a third contains the model forms of pension plans, wills, trusts, employment agreements, minutes, corporate bylaws, and a variety of miscellaneous agreements. Changes to documentation are fast and simple to execute. More than one operator can have access to the disk file for the same document model at the same time. Secretaries can continue to keyboard material into the system while the line printer and dedicated typewriter turn out previously stored material.

PROCEDURES. Work is received by the secretaries in two forms. An attorney will either mark up a model document by hand, with changes, deletions, and additions, or use a type of flow chart on which the blanks are filled in by hand with variable data. In either format, the model is identified by a code that corresponds to numbers identifying the copy stored on the magnetic disk. The operator enters the identification code on the typewriter keyboard, and then enters the changes shown on the marked-up document by typing out each indicated change or addition. The system automatically locates the section, makes the change, and adjusts the margins. With the flow-chart form, the system automatically types out questions for the operator to answer. Each reply triggers another typewritten inquiry, stepping the operator through all of the variables required by the form.

Shorter documents are typed either as originals or drafts and are also stored on disks, with numbers assigned to each document and paragraph. When corrections or revisions are needed, the system retrieves the document and paragraph in less than a second. Material can thus be easily revised several times. The system stores the updated version for instant retrieval. On command, the final version is produced on a 210-line-per-minute printer or on a 175-word-per-minute slave typewriter. The line printer is used for lengthy documents such as pension plans and the slave typewriter for trusts, wills, correspondence, and some pension plans. If the dedicated slave typewriter has a heavy backlog to turn out, one of the other typewriter terminals is used also as an unattended output station, while the secretary edits text or types entries into the system on the silent video keyboard.

PRODUCTIVITY. The system has dramatically reduced document production backlogs and improved service to clients. Documents can be prepared in one week instead of three, and tight deadlines no longer disrupt the entire office. In one instance, clients wished to enter into an agreement with a contractor to construct a medical building at a fixed price. The fact that the contracts and related papers could be prepared literally overnight permitted them to do so.

Production and management information is also built into the system. Access to a document file provides information on the current status and the amount of work in progress for a client, which can then be used for billing purposes. Another advantage of the system is the solid base of client data being developed from which a personalized mass mailing can be sent—for example, reporting new developments such as changes in pension regulations that directly affect particular clients.

Case Study
No. 12 Houston, Texas

Houston Lighting & Power Company[13]

BACKGROUND. Houston Lighting & Power Company is a privately owned electric utility serving over 2 million users in the Houston area. The specialized needs of several departments were formerly met by a word processing center equipped with seven Redactron magnetic card and tape typewriters. The credit department, for example, keeps a book of about 100 standard collection and information letters, each with a code number, and sends to the word processing center a daily list of names and code numbers for letters to customers. From 5,000 to 13,000 letters a month are produced, at an approximate cost of ten cents per letter. The information systems department writes and updates over 9,000 pages of systems and operating manuals for HL&P, making use of magnetic card equipment; magnetic cards each contain one page of a manual and are filed in page order. Dual magnetic card typewriters turn out fuel contracts, management reports, and correspondence for some nuclear report operations. The word processing center was well organized and productive with equipment suited to the work performed.

As a result of HL&P's involvement with nuclear-powered generating plants, the word processing operation changed. The Atomic Energy Commission (AEC) requires the production of Preliminary Safety Analysis Reports (PSARs) when construction of an atomic power station is proposed. During the preparation effort for the company's first atomic installation at Allen's Creek, HL&P learned that the physical volume of information required was impressive. The PSAR totaled 11 volumes containing 4,100 pages. Typing it required two months, 24 hours a day, by an outside word processing service at a cost of $90,000. The document

---

[13] "Job Matched Machines Boost Output and Economy," *Modern Office Procedures* (November 1974).

had to be completed within a rigid time frame; a similar schedule is required for revisions and replies to complex questions posed by the AEC. New questions and answers and amendments have increased the original 11 volumes to 18. An amendment can range from 50 to 1,800 pages.

In view of the effort and cost involved in the first project, a detailed study of the particular demands of this type of document was made when HL&P started to plan a second nuclear power plant. The goal for HL&P was a word processing system that could handle massive volumes of text editing and revision typing, with fast turnaround time to meet deadlines. Additional staff was not part of the plan. Therefore, the word processing center staff would have to learn the system and how to operate the new equipment quickly and easily.

STAFF AND EQUIPMENT. After detailed cost analysis, HL&P selected a minicomputer-based CRT text-editing system (described in detail in Chapter 7). The preparation of PSAR documents constitutes almost the entire activity of four 3M/Linolex units. The units each have three cassette drives, with a storage rate of 150,000 characters per cassette. Each unit is completely programmable by cassettes. Before starting work, the operator loads the program cassette into the first drive. The third drive takes a fresh cassette to record the new typed input. The second drive is a playback-only, for use in editing or in the duplicating mode of operation.

Operators work faster because program controls include first line of a page, last line, pagination, tab sets, and margins. As the operator keyboards words into the machine, they appear instantaneously on the CRT video screen, and a lighted arrow, as well as an operator guide, shows the typist the location on the page. Everything drafted is seen on the screen, where errors are easy to catch and correct before the operator calls for a printout. After running an index on the completed work, the recorded cassette is filed in the word processing center.

PROCEDURES. Input is supplied by technical staff—architects, engineers, and outside consultants, and the source material is divided and drafted according to AEC guidelines. The HL&P licensing section coordinates the entire report, logging and checking each chapter against work schedules and deadlines. Technical writers then edit, correct, and mark format instructions, before returning it to the word processing center. After the operator keyboards the material, the printed-out pages go to proofreaders and then back to the technical writers for approval. A review committee of HL&P management and engineering and environmental consultants makes a final inspection of the PSAR document before it is printed and submitted to the AEC.

PRODUCTIVITY. Peak workloads occur the month before the deadline for the document's submission. Most of the final typing takes place then. During the PSAR preparation for the South Texas project, the word processing center produced 11,904 pages in 37 days. The final printed report added up to 2,918 pages of text and 751 pages of figures. Also submitted was a 100-page application for license also prepared in the word processing center. By matching the right equipment to the demands of the PSAR preparation, the company realized a saving of $50,000 and obtained the internal control needed to assure the meeting of AEC deadlines. As a result of increasing work requirements, HL&P has established a separate satellite center for the credit and information systems departments, and has added four more CRT units to the word processing center for the PSAR operation.

After describing two applications of minicomputer-based word processing in the last two case studies, we shall now consider computer word processing in greater detail. The next chapter provides some historic background on the evolution of computers and the development of computer word processing.

SUGGESTED READINGS

"Del Monte Packs Quality in Word Processing," *Infosystems*, June 1974, pp. 66–67.

EVERHART, NINA R. "Technical Word Processing at Chevron-Geophysical Div.," *The Office*, February 1976, pp. 68–70.

"Job Matched Machines Boost Output and Economy," *Modern Office Procedures*, November 1974.

KRAEMER, JEANNE A. "Mountainside Hospital's Inventive Approach," *Word Processing*, July/August 1975, pp. 12–14.

"Library of Congress Steps into Word Processing," *Government Executive*, July 1975.

MARINELLI, DOLORES T. "Matching the Industry Gait," *Word Processing*, July/August 1975, pp. 3–5.

O'NEAL, JEFFREY D. "We Increased Typing Productivity 340%," *The Office*, February 1976, pp. 95–96, 98, 100.

PRIMROSE, BETTE. "Coordinated WP Yields Big Savings and High Morale," *Administrative Management*, November 1975, pp. 22–23, 58.

REYNOLDS, DAVID L. "An In-house Word Processing System," *Law Office Economics and Management*, Vol. XVI, No. 3, Fall 1975, pp. 436–440.

TUNKEL, PRISCILLA. "Central Dictation System Triples Typing Output over Four Year Period," *Corporate Systems*, October 1975.

"Washington Innovates to Cope with Paperwork," *Business Week*, June 30, 1975, p. 50.

"Word Processing Environment at Crown Center Hotel," *The Secretary*, October 1973.

"A W. R. Grace & Co. Word Processing Center," *The Office*, February 1976, pp. 28, 30, 32.

Chapter 7
COMPUTER WORD PROCESSING

Modern word processing began in the 1960s with the introduction of the IBM Selectric typewriter, a radically different electric typewriter with a ball element containing the type. The Selectric was developed originally as a device for transmitting and receiving data from a computer. When, as an input and output device, it is wired to a computer, it is known as a **computer terminal.** The terminals of modern computers are actually electric typewriters. The main terminal or **computer console has an electronic keyboard through which the computer operator enters program instructions and monitors the computer.** The computer in turn transmits signals through the keyboard to inform the operator when error conditions exist. (Another device used to prepare input data for the computer is the keypunch machine, which also has a typewriter-like keyboard.)

In addition to the main terminal, other typewriter terminals connected to a computer are used to automatically type out data stored in the computer and to keyboard by hand new data for storage. Thus the automatic typewriter is an integral part of electronic computers.[1] In data processing it is a terminal for data input, computations, and output. In word processing the automatic typewriter provides a keyboard for information input, editing, and output of written documents.

A brief review of the development of computers is needed at this point in order to provide background information for understanding the development of computer word processing. Since vocabulary used in this chapter deals with technical matters, the reader is advised to consult the glossary at the back of the book for a definition of any unfamiliar terms.

HISTORICAL DEVELOPMENT OF COMPUTERS

Electronic computers are the culmination of humankind's long search for a machine to perform calculations automatically. People's ability to perform mental arithmetic has never been as strong as their ability to reason, to think, and to invent. Perhaps the earliest and simplest calculating machine, believed to have originated in China about 2600 B.C., is the abacus. In the hands of a skilled operator, the abacus is still a versatile **digital** computer. On the other hand, the earliest **analog** computer, invented early in the seventeenth century, is the slide rule. Based on the logarithmic tables invented by John Napier, the slide rule performs multiplication and division by adding and subtracting.

The distinction between these concepts of digital and analog computations is an important one, as will be demonstrated in succeeding chapters. **Digital computers make exact numerical computations, but analog computers make approximate relational computations.** Common examples of these two differing modes of computing are the digital odometer and the analog speedometer in an automobile. The odometer measures the total number of miles the car has traveled. The speedometer measures the speed of the car in relation to the distance being covered within a specific time period. The digital computer operates sequentially, step by step, while the analog computer operates dynamically and continuously in a nonsequential process. In addition to digital and analog computers, there is a third type, a hybrid analog-digital computer, which is used by scientists and engineers.

At least four landmark events in the development of modern computers occurred in the nineteenth century. A direct forebearer of modern computers is the **analytical machine,** conceived by an English professor of mathematics, Charles Babbage, in the early nineteenth century. Borrowing the technique of perforated cards used to operate an automatic

---

[1] Richard McConnell and Pat Wells, "DP vs. WP," *Words* (Spring 1976), 11.

textile loom, **Babbage's machine had a memory unit as an integral part. The unit stored data in the form of holes punched in cards and combined arithmetic processes with decisions based on its own computations.** Unfortunately, Babbage's concept was too far in advance of the technology of the period, and his plans lay forgotten until 1937, when his writings were rediscovered.

Symbolic logic and the binary system of numbers that provide the basis for modern computer programming were developed in the mid-nineteenth century by the English logician and mathematician George Boole. The **binary system** used in digital computer calculations **is based on the digits 1 and 0, which combine to form numbers or plus and minus or yes and no.** Boole's concepts found application also in modern telephone communications and in computer switching theory and processes.

Another highly significant event was the appearance in 1873 of the first commercial typewriter, the Remington No. 1.

Late in the nineteenth century, a statistician with the U.S. Census Bureau became inspired, like Babbage, by punched cards. Herman Hollerith worked on the 1880 census using handwritten tally sheets, and the computations took over six years to complete. Realizing the need for a faster method, Hollerith invented a process of counting and sorting, using punched cards and electromagnetic devices that tabulated 200 items a minute. As a result of the new process, the 1890 census of 62 million people was completed in one third the time taken for the 1880 census of 50 million.

Hollerith's invention, which he only leased to the government, led to the development of a number of mechanical tabulating machines for commercial use. In time, Hollerith's punched card became the familiar IBM card in use today.

DEVELOPMENT OF ELECTRONIC COMPUTERS

The next landmark in the evolution of modern computers came in 1944, when Babbage's dream of the analytical machine was finally fulfilled by Howard Aiken of Harvard University. Aiken had become intrigued by Babbage's plan. Starting in 1939, he undertook a joint enterprise with a group of IBM engineers to complete the Automatic Sequence Controlled Calculator or the Mark I. Urgently needed to solve problems in military computations during World War II (1939–1945), the Mark I quickly led to additional automatic digital computers that incorporated many improvements.

Between 1942 and 1946, physicist John W. Mauchly and electrical engineer J. Presper Eckert developed the ENIAC or Electronic Numerical Integrator and Calculator at the University of Pennsylvania. The ENIAC required over 1,500 square feet of floor space. It was the first machine to use electronic tubes for calculating. Although designed chiefly for solving military problems in ballistics, the ENIAC contained advancements suitable for use in machines designed for business applications.

Eckert and Mauchly next developed a computer as a commercial venture, which they sold to Remington Rand. This was the UNIVAC or Universal Automatic Computer, which was installed in 1951 in the Census Bureau. It had a tabulating speed of 30,000 items a minute. The UNIVAC was also the first computer delivered to a business concern, General Electric in Louisville, Kentucky, where it was installed in 1954.

FIRST GENERATION OF COMMERCIAL COMPUTERS

The mid-1950s represent a transitional period in the history of computers. Many were designed expressly for business use and adapted to handling vast quantities of information typical of commercial operations. Although many large corporations acquired their first computers during the period 1953–1958, few firms justified the acquisition by cost effectiveness. The attitude at the time was that one had to acquire a computer in order to appear progressive.[2]

The computer had obvious application in financial areas, such as payroll, billing, and accounting; therefore, it usually became the responsibility of the chief financial officer or controller. In many organizations this relationship remains unchanged. Business management structures were affected by the need to accommodate computer personnel into the organization. The accommodation caused a disruption in traditional position rankings. Lack of rapport between computer professionals and operations people remains a problem in many companies up to the present time. The computer also had a negative effect on the morale of clerical workers who were concerned with the possibility of technological unemployment.[3]

SECOND GENERATION OF COMPUTERS

Technological advancements in electronics and solid-state physics resulted in the second generation of computers, which extended from about 1958 to 1966. Vacuum tubes were replaced by transistors, which were considerably smaller and more reliable. The result was a significant reduction in the physical size of computer systems, as well as vastly superior logic and core memories. Built-in error detection devices

---

[2] Frederic G. Withington, "Five Generations of Computers," *Harvard Business Review* (July-August 1974), p. 100.
[3] *Ibid.*

and better software were other improvements of the period. **Software refers to programming techniques or the set of instructions used to control the operations of a computer.** The first versions of universal operating systems for the purpose of scheduling the use of computer resources appeared toward the end of this period.[4]

The highly practical second-generation computers were designed to support the **batch processing** method, which is a **technique of collecting and grouping similar work for processing at one operation.** This method appeared the best way to handle large volumes of transactions. Everywhere that large quantities of information required routine processing, these computers and batch processing methods were found useful. No consideration was given to the overall logic or the evolution of these routine processing procedures. For instance, payroll programs for computers had been adapted from punched-card procedures, which had been adapted from accounting machine procedures, which in turn had been adapted from the manual procedures of the 1800s. Computer programs in many companies thus tended to continue methods developed for a slower mechanical era, rather than being logically planned to make full use of the computer's instantaneous electronic speed. This was true both in the routine processing of large volumes of data, and in the planning and decision-making for which top management used the computer as a souce of information.[5]

Two trail blazers in the development of modern computer applications based on rapid access to file data were airline reservation systems and stock quotation systems. Other computer users began demanding modern applications based on the incredible speed of computer calculations, in order to gain more rapid access to stored information. The development of **disk storage, which permits random access to individual transactions in a fraction of a second,** increased the printing speed of computer output units. Another new development was teleprocessing equipment to expedite the flow of information between computers over long distances. (See Chapter 8 for details.) As the applications of computers multiplied, the machines also multiplied. Some large corporations established several computer centers under the control of the production, distribution, or marketing departments, rather than under the chief financial officer. With increasing numbers of machines, the number of data processing personnel also increased at all levels, and their presence raised the nagging question of control over their work efforts within the office hierarchy.

Computers also made the period 1958–1966 a difficult one for clerical personnel, with positions such as billing clerk and check-sorting clerk

---

[4] *Ibid.*
[5] *Ibid.*

reduced or eliminated entirely. However, the computer often created as many jobs as it eliminated, as in key-punching and machine operations. Thus it resulted not in fewer clerical positions but in new clerical work patterns.

THIRD GENERATION OF COMPUTERS

The third generation of computer equipment (1966–1974) and the next major advance occurred with the introduction of micro-miniaturized integrated circuits. These smaller, faster, more reliable components are found in the IBM System/360, a general purpose family of computers ranging from small to very large models, capable of handling both business and scientific applications. (Although IBM is the giant of the computer industry, others in the field include Burroughs, Honeywell, Sperry Univac, NCR, and CDC.)

Third-generation computers are communicator computers. With lower costs and integrated circuits, new types of remote terminals became feasible. These remote terminals allow users in many dispersed locations to communicate with a centrally located computer. Recent surveys show that 90 percent of all large computers now have some remote terminals attached, usually by means of telephone lines.[6] Most large organizations are now using their computers as the central processing units of a communications network that connects widely dispersed operational sites. The central computers must handle many operations at once, break off current operations to receive and acknowledge messages, store many pending and partly finished jobs until time permits their completion, and ensure that every job gets done on schedule.

Unlike batch processing computers of the second generation that do one thing at a time, communicator computers are required to respond to many stimuli at unpredictable times. Thus, complicated systems and control programs were required to integrate the new computer components. Some of the other new components in addition to remote terminals include **optical scanners** and **magnetic ink character readers.** These devices **permit direct processing** by the **computer of bank checks, airline tickets, and similar documents, without human intervention.**

Third generation computers also introduced further complexities in the organization of many large corporations. When computer power was consolidated at the central unit, many divisional managers lost control of their internal data processing. At the same time, central management had to develop new structures to incorporate the functions of

---

[6] *Ibid.*, p. 102

the corporation-wide data processing and communications network. Specialists to develop appropriate computer programs resulted. The consequent need to locate these new computer professionals within the existing but changing organizational structures added to the complexity of the situation.[7]

A corporation-wide communications network places central management in a position to see detailed data on division operations as soon as, or even before, the divisional managers see it. In one retail chain, store managers dread Mondays because the previous week's profit statements are prepared for each store over the weekend by the central computer. Central management reviews them the first thing on Monday morning, and, if the results are unsatisfactory, store managers hear about it by telephone, often before they themselves have received the computer printout of the report.[8] Problems in procedures are not insurmountable, however, and are usually corrected in time, with people at all levels acknowledging the value of the up-to-the-minute, complete data supplied by the computer.

USE OF MINICOMPUTERS

Another significant development of the late 1960s was the minicomputer and its use as a remote terminal. Minicomputers are small computers, fast in computation, but with limited input, output, and secondary storage devices. When connected to larger computers, minicomputers can handle specialized functions that would only slow down the performance of the larger system. The first minicomputer was invented in 1964 by Digital Equipment Corporation. The minicomputer industry, which also includes IBM, Hewlett-Packard, and Wang Laboratories, became firmly established by bringing a relatively inexpensive intelligence (compared with a large computer) to the point of use. For instance, in a corporate data processing system, a central computer connects a corporate headquarters with one of its plants or factories. The factory office in turn is connected to a series of minicomputers at various locations in the plant. Each minicomputer is in control of a cluster of microcomputers, which in turn control the operations of a machine or a production line. (Microcomputers, developed in the 1970's, are described later in this chapter.) In this type of hierarchical system, each minicomputer operates on its own, sending data up the hierarchy and in turn receiving operating instructions from higher-ranking units. Minicomputers are expected by 1984 to control some 26 percent of automated

---

[7] *Ibid.*
[8] *Ibid.*, p. 103.

factory equipment, and microcomputers some 50 percent. In metalworking alone, expectations are that over 200 large, integrated systems of automation will be in operation.[9]

Just as the large computer has automated corporate operations such as payroll and accounting, minicomputers may do the same for general office operations at comparatively low cost. In 1974, the cost of a minicomputer was 39 percent less than in 1968, and by the 1980s the cost is expected to go down again by more than 50 percent.[10] A minicomputer runs about $50,000 for a standard business application; however, it handles much of the work of large computers that cost $2 million. Although they cost about one fortieth as much as a large computer, minicomputers can handle far more than one fortieth of the work.[11]

COMPUTER WORD PROCESSING

Following the introduction of the third generation communicator computers in the mid-1960s, IBM also produced a Communicating Mag Card Selectric Typewriter for use as a remote terminal for its IBM Systems 360, 370, and System 3 computers, as well as for use with compatible computer systems of other manufacturers. The communicating read/record console of the typewriter uses magnetic cards for recording, playout, or transmission. The console also permits the preparation of prerecorded magnetic cards for later playout as typewritten documents, for transmitting data by long distance to another Communicating Mag Card Selectric, or for providing access to the computer. This latter use, called **accessing, is the process of feeding in or extracting information from the computer.** The magnetic cards hold information in typewritten form, which is easily stored, changed, or inserted into other documents. Information contained on the magnetic cards can also be transmitted automatically from one location to another at high speed. Transmission is usually over telephone lines. The capability for high-speed transmission of documents from one Communicating Mag Card to another and the capability to operate as a remote computer terminal are combined in the same machine that is used to type correspondence. Computer data and transmitted documents are received at the other end in the form of typewritten printout on paper or as information recorded on magnetic cards or both. Magnetic card storage plus document transmission capability provide readily available management information.

The favorable growth outlook for such communicating word process-

---

[9] "Even the Smallest Machine Will Have Its Own 'Brain,'" *Business Week* (September 14, 1974), p. 171.

[10] *Ibid.*

[11] Gerald J. Burnett and Richard L. Nolan, "At Last, Major Roles for Minicomputers," *Harvard Business Review* (May-June 1975).

ing units is attributable to decreasing communications costs, rising mail costs, and the labor-intensive mail service. Other important factors include the possibility of getting fast response at remote locations or immediate action on written documents such as contracts, proposals, legal briefs, and ratifications. The value of communicating word processing units is enhanced by flexibility, since almost any two units can transmit and receive material between themselves; computers, TWX/Telex, and other makes of communicating typewriters are examples.

A large manufacturer with several plants located nationwide provides one case study of applied word processing communications. Research showed that 80 percent of its written communications stayed within the company. The system includes communicating typewriters at each plant, all linked to a central computer by means of company telephone tie lines. To send a message, a person dictates into the word processing center at one of the plants; the message is transcribed and recorded there on a magnetic card. After the transcribed message is approved by the originator, the word processing center transmits the contents of the magnetic card to the CPU (central processing unit of the computer), which batches and stores messages. When lines are free, the CPU dispatches messages to the intended plants, where they are received on magnetic cards. Then they are played out on the communicating typewriter. This kind of intracompany correspondence permits executives to take immediate action on pressing matters instead of waiting for mail delivery. It has also reduced mailroom requirements.[12]

TIME SHARE COMPUTING—
WORD PROCESSING AND DATA PROCESSING

Organizations with a need for computer capability in the handling of text editing and high-quality typeset page requirements can gain the benefits of a computer without installing their own in-house computer system. Similarly, organizations with in-house computers that are overscheduled and have programming backlogs can find relief on a temporary or permanent basis. One possible solution for both problems is **time-share computing. Limited segments of an out-of-house computer** (usually the large IBM 360 series) **and computer-related services can be purchased from time-sharing service bureaus.** A typewriter terminal in the user's office is connected to the computer through normal telephone lines. The time sharing computer is a multiprogramming, multiprocessing, and multiple-access computer that can be operated by many users simultaneously.[13]

---

[12] "WP: Path to the '80s," *Modern Office Procedures* (June 1975), p. 98.
[13] Norman H. Wright, Jr., "Time Share Computing," *Management World* (May 1975), p. 10.

Costs for time sharing include the terminal, connection time, storage, CPU usage, printout charges, and phone charges. The system operates on the basis of "pay as you use it." One big advantage of computer word processing from a time-sharing service is the use of the software programs supplied by the service without the need for employing a skilled in-house computer operator. A number of standard data processing programs for accounts receivable, accounts payable, or payroll systems are usually available to the users at no additional charge. Another advantage in word processing applications is that original documents can be typed and edited **on line,** which means **the user is directly accessing the computer's CPU.** The documents are then printed on high-speed printers or photocomposition devices at the central computer location, and delivered by messenger the next day. The input terminal and the operator are not tied up for extended periods in the process.[14]

Time-sharing computer service provides greater computer power and flexibility than a single user can obtain otherwise. It handles peak and valley workloads economically. In addition, one computer service will often serve the needs of engineering, production, and financial users.[15]

MINICOMPUTER WORD PROCESSING SYSTEMS

Since 1971, minicomputer systems totally dedicated to word processing have been introduced by a number of manufacturers. The central processing unit has a minicomputer instead of a large computer, with typewriter terminals or CRT video devices used for input, and typewriter terminals or medium- to high-speed printers for output. Storage devices include tape-drives or random-access floppy disk units. A **floppy disk** is **a form of magnetic recording media used in word processing and data processing** to distinguish it from the rigid disks that are also used in computer memories. The floppies permit **random access** to stored data so that rapid search and retrieval is possible regardless of where the data is located on the disk. In contrast, magnetic tape provides **serial storage** of data in a set sequence, which usually means a longer search time.

Unlike the large computer systems that employ remote terminals, the units of a minicomputer word processing system are usually located on the same premises. The input terminals, ranging in number from three to fifteen, are usually wired directly to the minicomputer instead of utilizing telephone lines for transmission. These systems are particularly effective where volumes of lengthy documents with extensive editing are required, where voluminous legal documents in large numbers are

---

[14] Charles Cumpston, "Automated Typing Systems Move the Words Out Faster," Word Processing Management Section of *Administrative Management* (June 1973), p. 52.

[15] Wright, *op. cit.*, p. 11

FIGURE 7-1
The DEC (Digital Equipment Corporation) DATASYSTEM 310W is a powerful, minicomputer-based word and data processing system. An operator console, the DECscope, contains a keyboard and video display terminal that sits upon a desk containing the system's minicomputer and dual disk drives. A separate desk wing contains a Xerox/Diablo wheelprinter.

needed, or where prestructured paragraphs are used in correspondence. With the addition of a photocomposition component, these minicomputer systems create camera-ready typeset-quality documents.

MANUFACTURERS OF MINICOMPUTER WORD PROCESSING SYSTEMS

With the trend toward combining word processing and data processing into a management information system, some of the newest minicomputer systems offer software for both word processing and data processing applications. **Software** refers to computer programs or sets of instructions to control the computer **hardware,** which is the machinery.

Digital Equipment Corporations's Datasystem 310W (Figure 7–1) performs data processing tasks such as payroll, order processing, accounts payable and receivable, inventory control, sales analysis, and more. When used as a word processing system, the 310W expedites the production of contracts, sales proposals, direct-mail letters and lists, engineering documents, and so on. The 310W features dual floppy disk drives for unlimited data and program storage. Each 8 × 8-inch floppy disk can store over 100 pages of text. The dual disk drives provide for one disk containing the stored operating instructions or program for the computer, and for a second disk with the specific data or text application. To change the system from a word processor to a data processor, all that is needed is to change the floppy program disk. With the push of a button, either the text-editing software or the data processing software is loaded into the system's memory and is ready to use.

There is no complicated computer language to learn in operating the 310W because of its turnkey software. **Turnkey software** signifies that **the computer program provides the operator with complete instructions**

FIGURE 7-2
LCS Corporation's basic Compu-TEXT cluster, a complete typing system, consists of a video typing station, an electronic printer, and a module containing a single disk drive over a DEC minicomputer. The basic cluster is expandable to four disk drives and eight typing stations.

for operating the system. Cue "cards" and "menu" lists are displayed on the video terminal with instructions for the operator. The menu gives features of the system; cue cards show the operator how to utilize the system. The basic 310W system consists of a CRT terminal for visual text-editing, a powerful central processing unit to control system operation, dual floppy-disk drives, and a letter-quality printer. The 310W, which costs approximately $22,500, also has the capability of communicating with another similar system or a centralized computer.

LCS Corporation's Compu-TEXT (Figure 7-2), a computer typing system, is one of the leaders in the field of minicomputer-based word processing. Modular units, available as standard components, provide low-cost expansion and system flexibility. A basic Compu-TEXT cluster consists of a video typing station, an electronic printer, and a single disk drive with a floppy disk that has a storage capacity of 1,000 pages. A DEC minicomputer supplies the central processing unit in the Compu-TEXT system.

The basic cluster can be expanded up to four disk storage units and up to eight typing stations. Different applications are handled simultaneously, whether revisions, transcription, automatic letters, or mass mailings. The electronic typing stations play out at 540 words per minute, and an optional high-speed printer plays out at 4400 words per minute. Another option, the Compu-TEXT Autoreader is an **optical character recognition** (OCR) scanner. An **OCR is a device that scans a page of copy originally typed on a regular Selectric typewriter and then automatically feeds it into the word processing system.** The OCR thus eliminates the need for re-keyboarding material typed on regular Selectric typewriters. It provides a fast, easy way to convert output from any nonautomatic Selectric machines in an office for processing by the automatic machines.

Depending on the optional peripheral equipment selected, an LCS installation ranges from approximately $60,000 to $150,000.

Data-Text, a product of General Computer Systems, is a more advanced and more powerful type of shared logic system. A **shared logic system is one in which several keyboard terminals use the memory and processing powers of the same computer's central processing unit at the same time.** Data-Text, with up to 32 video display terminal keyboards connected to a minicomputer, can handle a whole range of text manipulations. The terminals also communicate data to a remote computer and perform a variety of electronic data processing functions. What is more, these operations are all handled simultaneously.[16]

---

[16] Belden Menkus, "Multi-Function Word Processors: A Step Beyond Shared Logic," *Administrative Management* (March 1974).

FIGURE 7-3
A triumph of miniaturization is represented in these pictures of old and new computers. The first electronic digital computer, called ENIAC, below, was completed in 1946 and had 18,000 vacuum tubes which had to function simultaneously. ENIAC's power source (not shown) occupied about half as much space as the computer itself. The Intel 8080 "chip-on-a-finger" microcomputer shown at right exceeds ENIAC in computational ability.

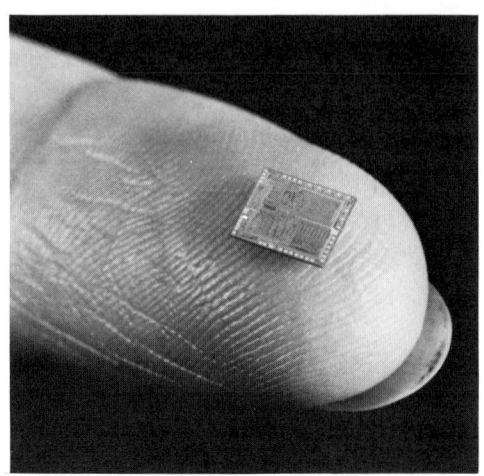

Other multifunction word processing systems using minicomputers include the 3M/Linolex 4000 Word Processor, the Eldorado 14 from Eldorado Computer, and the Comptek Accutext from Comptex Research. A more extensive list of manufacturers in this rapidly growing field is offered in an appendix.

MICROCOMPUTERS AND THE SECOND COMPUTER REVOLUTION

Three generations of technological change show computers continuously evolving as smaller, faster, and more powerful. Thirty years ago, ENIAC contained some 18,000 vacuum tubes, weighed thirty tons, and sprawled over 1,500 square feet. Despite its size, ENIAC started the computer revolution by performing 5,000 additions or subtractions a second. Vacuum tubes gave way to transistors in the second generation of computers; and, in the third generation, transistors were replaced by integrated circuits. Computer speed changed from fifteen calculations a second with vacuum tubes to 400,000 a second with the first integrated circuits.[17]

A second computer revolution started in 1971 with the invention of the microprocessor by a young engineer, M. E. Hoff, Jr., of Intel Corporation. The microprocessor is based on the development of monolithic systems technology or MST. MST is an outgrowth of the earlier solid logic technology, which provided the basis for the first integrated circuits. MST made possible microscopic logic circuits that perform over one million calculations a second.[18]

Hoff's **microprocessor is a single chip of silicon containing the "brain" or central processing unit of a computer.** Hoff attached to the CPU chip two memory chips: one moves data in and out of the CPU, and the other provides the program to drive the CPU. Smaller than a cube of sugar, Hoff's tiny microcomputer is just as powerful as the thirty-ton ENIAC.[19]

Computers are unique machines because of their ability to perform many different tasks based on a stored yet alterable program. The microcomputer can now impart this ability to other mechanical devices. In addition, its program can be changed simply by replacing a tiny memory chip with a different one. Thus, a standard microcomputer system makes possible large economies in manufacturing. The same system can be used for many different products simply by using a differ-

---

[17] "Computers: A New Wave," *Newsweek*, (February 23, 1976), p. 73.
[18] *Ibid.*
[19] Gene Bylinsky, "Here Comes the Second Computer Revolution," *Fortune*, (November 1975), p. 136.

ent program chip. The microcomputer both reduces costs and enhances the product's capabilities and value. Electric typewriters, cash registers, microwave ovens, traffic lights, and complex scientific instruments are some of the products already enhanced by microcomputers.[20]

A second-generation microcomputer produced by Intel Corporation, the 8080, is twenty times faster than its first model, the 4040. The 8080 begins to match a minicomputer in its computational speed. It has the capability to control a computer printer or a whole series of them, thereby eliminating an electromechanical relay or hard-wired logic systems. The microcomputer on a chip has simplified the complex, rigid design of electronic computers and provides for more generalized flexible applications in computer technology.[21]

MICROCOMPUTER WORD PROCESSING SYSTEMS

Microcomputers are used in the second-generation CRT word processing systems as described in Chapter 2. CRT microcomputer systems have the potential to communicate with standard computer word processing systems as well as with other microcomputer systems. The microcomputer has made these word processing machines easier to operate than the earlier automatic typewriters because of its powerful data processing capacity in programming the machine to perform complex operations. The skill formerly needed by the operator now is programmed into the machine.

SUGGESTED READINGS

BURNETT, GERALD J., and RICHARD L. NOLAN. "At Last, Major Roles for Minicomputers," *Harvard Business Review*, May-June 1975.

BYLINSKY, GENE. "Here Comes the Second Computer Revolution," *Fortune*, November 1975, pp. 135–139, 182, 184.

"Computers: A New Wave," *Newsweek*, February 23, 1976, pp. 73–74.

CUMPSTON, CHARLES. "Automated Typing Systems Move the Words Out Faster," Word Processing Management Section of *Administrative Management*, June 1973, pp. 41–52.

"Even the Smallest Machine Will Have Its Own 'Brain,' "*Business Week*, September 14, 1974, pp. 171–172.

McCONNELL, RICHARD, and PAT WELLS. "DP vs. WP," *Words*, Spring 1976, p. 11.

---

[20] *Ibid.*, p. 135.
[21] *Ibid.*, pp. 137–138.

MENKUS, BELDEN. "Multi-Function Word Processors: A Step Beyond Shared Logic," *Administrative Management*, March 1974, pp. 48, 50, 52, 54–55.

WITHINGTON, FREDERIC G. "Five Generations of Computers," *Harvard Business Review*, July-August 1974, pp. 99–108.

"WP: Path to the '80s," *Modern Office Procedures*, June 1975, pp. 93–99.

WRIGHT, NORMAN H., Jr. "Time Share Computing," *Management World*, May 1975, pp. 9–11.

Chapter 8

WORD PROCESSING AND MANAGEMENT INFORMATION SYSTEMS

Theoretically, a management information system (MIS) has three major segments: data processing, word processing, and executive control. The executive control function covers organizational activity involved in the initiation of, or response to, the data and word processing functions. Of the three information management segments, executive control and word processing are significantly less automated at present than the data processing function. The next logical step toward achieving an actual management information system is further integration of the word processing segment as an automatic function in order thereby to create opportunities for automation in the executive control segment.[1]

If the office is viewed as a complex communications network using written words as the pri-

---

[1] Kenneth W. Ford, "The Management of Information," *The Office* (September 1974), p. 19.

mary form of communication, word processing, by generating documents in a cost-efficient automated manner, becomes a major component of the network.[2] However, in the generation of written words, other communications-related problems exist that are not currently covered by word processing systems. A broader approach to the information flow in a company expands the word processing concept to encompass not only generating words or information but also disseminating and storing information for use in the most cost-effective way.[3]

An integrated system for automated office communications requires that word processing and related technologies combine in a multimedia environment of information-handling and management. The total word processing cycle consists not only of originating a document and frequently revising and retyping it, but also of disseminating it, and, when it is received, evoking a response—thus repeating the cycle.[4] Therefore, the functional areas of a word processing system are: originating, production, and utilization. **Originating** is the creating of words or information. **Production** is the typing and distributing of information. **Utilization** is the process of reading the words when received, acting upon them, and then storing them for further reference.[5] A multitude of media, machines, and other devices are currently available to facilitate each step of the word processing cycle.

Media that contain words for distribution include: longhand or shorthand words written on paper; printed words on paper; vocal or digital code recordings of words on magnetic tape, disk, or belt; video display screens; and photographic images on film.[6] Machines include dictation equipment, electric or automatic typewriters, communicating typewriters, copiers, high-speed printers, photo-composition units. Other devices include microfilm, telephones, switchboards, telephone and telegraph lines, private data transmission lines, TWX and Telex, Mailgrams, and facsimile.

The first originating step in the word processing cycle usually involves the use of dictation equipment. The second production step requires keyboarding of words and preparing multiple copies through the use of typewriters, copiers, printers, offset press, and/or microfilm. Distribution is made (1) by messenger or (2) by mail or (3) by electronic mail transmitted over telephone or private data transmission lines or Western Union lines as Mailgrams, TWX and Telex, or facsimile or two communicating typewriters or by computer to a remote terminal. The third step in

---

[2] John W. Mitchell, "New Direction for WP: The Communications Management Department," *Word Processing Report* (June 1, 1975).

[3] *Ibid.*

[4] Ford, *op. cit.*, p. 20.

[5] *Ibid.*

[6] *Ibid.*

the word processing cycle involves procedures for making additional copies for further distribution and for storing, retrieving, or destroying the document. Before storing, the document is indexed and possibly transformed to another medium such as microfilm.

The many devices used in the distribution and utilization of information, therefore, are closely related to word processing systems and fall under the general categories of telecommunications and records management. A brief consideration of recent technological developments in telecommunications and records management is vital in understanding why their integration with word processing systems will eventually lead to executive control and an overall management information system.

TELECOMMUNICATIONS

Telecommunications is a science that deals with the study of communication at a distance as, for instance, by cable, radio, telegraph, telephone, or television. Significant developments in the field of telecommunications have been due to the rapid spread of electronic computers and the need for transmitting data between computers and their remote terminals or between two or more widely separated communicating typewriters. The nation's telephone network is particularly affected, since telephone lines are used to transmit information by computers and by communicating word processing machines. Following is a survey of recent developments in data transmission (including electronic mail, facsimile, TWX/Telex, Mailgrams) and also in computerized office telephone switchboards, which shows their significance in relation to management information systems.

DATA TRANSMISSION NETWORKS. The telephone lines of American Telephone & Telegraph Company (AT&T), the world's largest corporation, and its 24 operating companies that make up the Bell System are used not only for long distance telephone calls but also for information and data transmission by computers, by communicating typewriters, by facsimile, and by teleprinters. AT&T's network, however, is designed to carry the fluctuating *analog* tones of the human voice, not the rapid, rat-a-tat signals of the *digital*-computer code. (The important distinction between analog and digital computers is discussed in Chapter 7.) Before they are sent over telephone lines, the digital signals must first be encoded into analog signals and later decoded at the receiving end. The device that performs this function is called a **modem, a contraction for "modulator-demodulator."** As a result of this process, errors are frequent and transmission speeds relatively slow.[7] Consequently, after

---

[7] Gene Bylinsky, "Datran's Hazardous High-Wire Act," *Fortune* (February 1976), p. 131.

receiving large numbers of complaints from customers and the computer industry over the operating deficiencies of the Bell System's basic voice network, the Federal Communications Commission (FCC) licensed a number of specialized carriers to build data transmission systems. Datran, founded in 1968, Microwave Communications, Inc., and others were licensed by the FCC in 1971 to build both terrestrial and satellite networks in competition with AT&T.

In 1972, AT&T announced plans to use microwave channels for the digital transmission of data. By installing digital transmitters and receivers in its existing analog microwave system, AT&T planned to create a data network located under the analog or voice band. However, this "data-under-voice" network would not provide a switching service for connecting any computer terminal on the network with any other terminal. Customers therefore had to lease expensive full-time private lines to connect their remote computer terminals.[8] The new AT&T data network, called Dataphone Digital Service, is expected to serve 96 cities throughout the country at price reductions to match AT&T's competitors in the long distance communications business. The computer time-sharing systems discussed in Chapter 7 are users of Dataphone as are other organizations with big data networks.

Meanwhile, construction of a brand-new nationwide network for data transmission was underway, to compete with AT&T. Starting from scratch, Datran (Data Transmission Company) planned a network functioning in the digital mode in the hope of cutting transmission errors to one one-hundredth of the Bell System's, speeding up the flow of data, and substantially reducing costs. Also in the plans was **a switching system** that would **permit computer terminals anywhere on the network to be connected with one another almost instantaneously**.[9] Financial difficulties made necessary Datran's gradual accommodation with AT&T as well as changes in the original plan. By leasing certain facilities from AT&T and Southern Pacific, and by constructing others, Datran now offers a switched digital service along a network that stretches coast-to-coast. All calls on the Datran switched network go to the computerized switch near Chicago, which directs them and completes the connection in less than one second. By comparison, connection time on AT&T's analog network ranges from 11 to 17 seconds. A Datran customer can transmit some 2,500 words to a terminal 600 miles distant in 10 seconds, and pay only 3 cents for the call.[10] Datran's digital network is shown in Figure 8–2.

One Datran customer, American Hospital Supply Corporation, has facilities in 32 states and makes more than 3000 data calls a day. The

---

[8] *Ibid.*, p. 133.
[9] *Ibid.*, p. 131.
[10] *Ibid.*, p. 139

Telecommunications 123

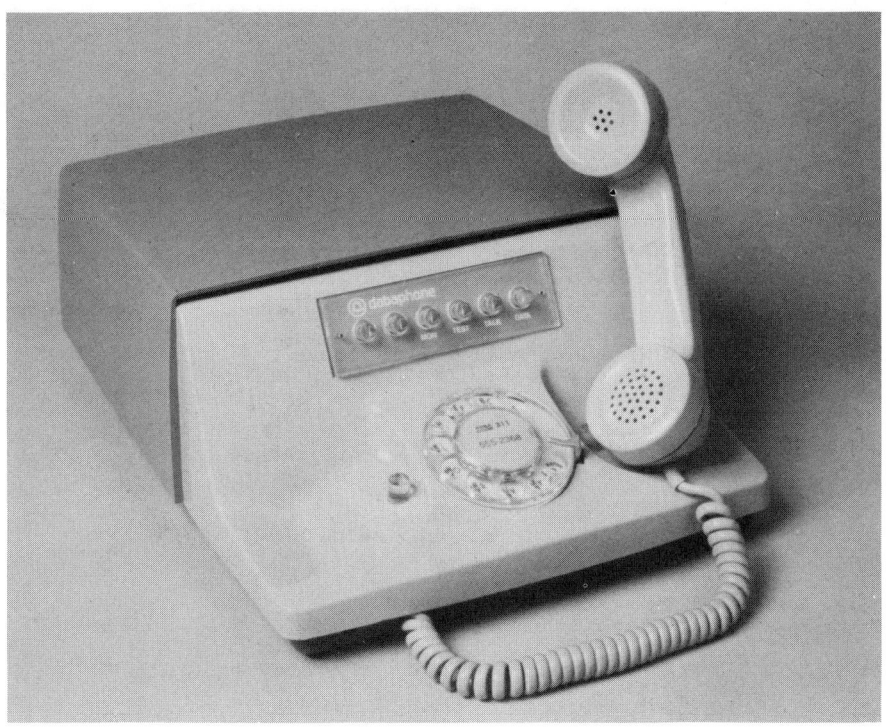

FIGURE 8-1
Dataphone used to connect computer terminals on the new AT&T data transmission network.

company's highly evolved computerized management information system helps to control production and inventories. The company is also developing a new system to allow its sales representatives to answer customers' questions immediately by pressing buttons and receiving information on a CRT video display screen. With the Datran system, one inquiry can cost as little as one cent. As computers continue to proliferate, the demand for data transmission services will proliferate, as will the need for reliable, fast, error-free transmission in the digital computer mode.

As this book goes to press, Datran filed for voluntary bankruptcy after losses totalling nearly $100 million. The day before announcing its shutdown, Datran filed an antitrust suit against AT&T for triple damages of $285 million. Recent rate hearings held by the FCC indicate that AT&T's pricing on digital data transmission was "anti-competitive" and "unlawful." AT&T, however, maintains that its rates, although 40 percent below Datran's, are based on an analysis of actual costs and risks. FCC characterizes the competitive response of AT&T to Datran as "predatory"

FIGURE 8-2   DATA TRANSMISSION SERVICES

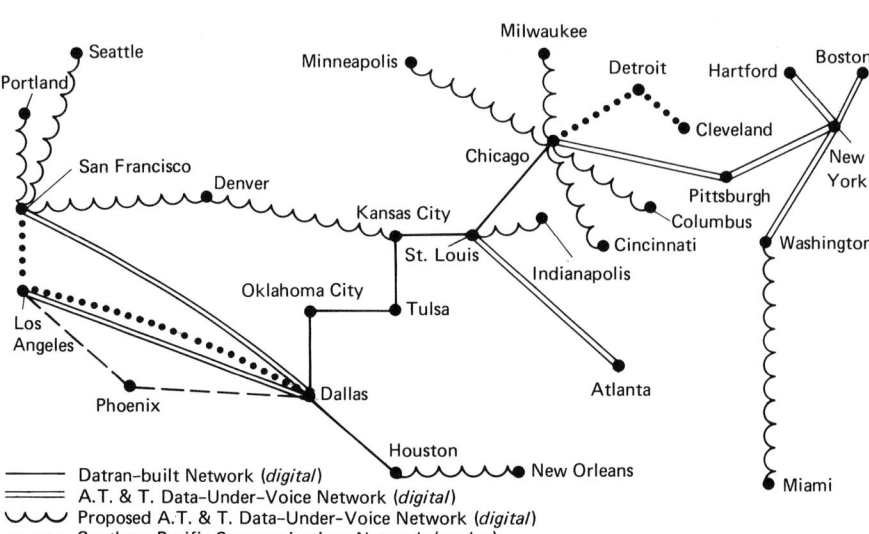

——— Datran-built Network (*digital*)
=== A.T. & T. Data-Under-Voice Network (*digital*)
ᴗᴗᴗ Proposed A.T. & T. Data-Under-Voice Network (*digital*)
••••• Southern Pacific Communications Network (*analog*)
— — — Proposed Southern Pacific Communications Network (*analog*)

Source: Gene Bylinsky, "Datran's Hazardous High-Wire Act," *Fortune* (February 1976), 133.

and the reason Datran could not raise needed financing for its private line transmission service. (Source: "A Shocking Failure in Communications," *Business Week*, September 6, 1976, p. 22.)

FACSIMILE. Another office machine—namely, facsimile or fax—transmits data and information over long distances by means of telephone lines. A connection between two offices is first made by a telephone call. The person at the receiving end then turns on the fax and receives an exact copy, one page at a time, of the material fed into the distant fax by the sender. Facsimile provides copies not only of typed pages but of diagrams, charts, sketches, and handwritten documents, as well.

Datran is competing with AT&T in facsimile transmission by test marketing a digital facsimile machine that can send letter-size documents cross-country in twenty-five seconds. In large volume the cost per page is 15 cents. The Xerox plain-paper Telecopier presently uses analog transmission on ordinary telephone lines to send documents long distance. The Telecopier combines a laser with xerography; but, at the transmission rate of two minutes per page, long distance telephone charges can be expensive. Datran plans to provide an advanced digital facsimile machine, produced by an outside manufacturer, that may lead to the real start of electronic mail for large corporations. At present, however, facsimile is being used by increasing numbers of Washington law firms that order a Telecopier as they would a telephone.[11] Leading suppliers in the facsimile market are Xerox, 3M, Graphic Sciences, and Stewart-Warner, with Dacom and Rapifax also making strong progress.[12]

In 1975 a technical marketing research firm, the Yankee Group of Cambridge, Massachusetts, found that 50 percent of all facsimile messages are transmitted a distance of from 1 to 50 miles, and another 35 percent up to 500 miles; 92 percent of all messages are sent intracompany. To date, therefore, the point-to-point use of facsimile is not a substitute for the broadcast nature of Western Union's TWX and Telex network. Within a few years some 500 million messages a year will probably be sent by facsimile. New features providing for reduced transmission time and unattended operation will make facsimile even more competitive. The nonreliance of business firms on the U.S. Postal Service is another strong stimulant to the growth of facsimile.[13]

ELECTRONIC MAIL. The legal division of the Internal Revenue Service has a network of communicating typewriters linking thirty field offices. Legal briefs drafted in the field formerly were mailed to the Washington headquarters for review; however, the slowness of mail deliveries and the increasing volume of tax cases made it difficult for IRS lawyers to meet court dates. Now, the network of communicating typewriters makes it possible to transmit a brief in digital mode over telephone lines to IRS headquarters, where the machine types out a duplicate copy and stores the brief on magnetic tape at the same time. In case the Dallas field office, for instance, requests a copy of a brief for a tax case, the stored text is easily sent from Washington at high speed to a communicating typewriter in Dallas, where it is automatically typed out, error-free, as an original document. Since facsimiles are not accepted by the courts, this form of electronic mail has a special advantage in legal use.[14]

Federal agencies were among the earliest users of word processing equipment, and innovative applications of electronic mail networks are growing in Washington at a prodigious rate. Estimates of word processing typewriters alone installed in federal offices are expected to be 81,500 by 1980.[15] A word processing system installed by the Navy Recruit-

---

[11] "The Office of the Future," *Business Week* (June 30, 1975), p. 56.
[12] "Facsimile Usage to Pick Up Steam in Next Two Years," *Infosystems* (September 1975), p. 33.
[13] *Ibid.*
[14] "Washington Innovates to Cope with Paperwork," *Business Week* (June 30, 1975), p. 50.
[15] *Ibid.*

ing Command links 198 communicating typewriters and 150 dictation units at 78 locations nationwide to the headquarters office in Arlington, Virginia. The network permits communication among the machines themselves as well as with the Arlington office. The Navy formerly used Telecopiers which required six minutes to transmit one page over telephone lines. A drastic reduction in telephone charges is expected with the new system, which can transmit 12 pages in three minutes. The cost for the Navy's system is $1.5 million. Because it will allow a reduction in staff, the word processing system is expected to save some $4.6 million annually and provide point-to-point communications that meet the Navy's need for data on a timely basis. Similar systems are under consideration by the Army, the Agriculture Department, the Social Security Administration, and other divisions of the Internal Revenue Service.[16]

Computers linked to communicating typewriters are also used for high-speed electronic mail. The typewriter terminal transmits the contents of a magnetic card to the central processing unit of a computer, that can either transmit the message instantaneously or can **batch and store** messages until the receiving terminal and line are free to receive. In a telephone network, this feature is known as **store and forward.** Store and forward provides for improved utilization of computer lines, rapid delivery, and reduced mailroom requirements.

MAILGRAMS. Western Union's Mailgram service also employs a store and forward process, which is technically called **message switching.** Each Mailgram message received from customers during the day is stored in the central processing unit of Western Union's computer for transmission during the night to a teleprinter or teletypewriter located at the post office nearest to the Mailgram's addressee. Upon receipt, the Mailgram is inserted into a window envelope and dispatched by the postal service in the first mail delivery the next morning.

Mailgram is a coordinated form of private and public electronic mail provided by Western Union in cooperation with the U.S. Postal Service. Apart from the Mailgram service, postal authorities have shown little interest in setting up electronic mail systems. The need for fast, efficient document distribution is an overwhelming business need that the deteriorating postal service is not meeting. Electronic mail will be a major component in future office systems.

TWX AND TELEX. TWX and Telex stand for the teletypewriter and teleprinter exchange service of Western Union. A teleprinter is operated by a teletypist who phones another teletypist at a distant location; once the connection is made, the two teletypists communicate by typing back and forth while the machines record their messages in writing. Typing

---

[16] *Ibid.*

actions are converted into electrical pulses that produce a printed telegraph system. The TWX/Telex network takes in some 225,000 installations at major business locations across the U.S., Canada, and Mexico. The network is used by large companies for communications inside and outside their organizations. TWX/Telex machines can communicate also with communicating typewriters and computers, but their operation is expected to prove vulnerable to the high-speed transmission and automation provided by the newest types of facsimile equipment.

OFFICE TELEPHONE SWITCHBOARDS. Computer technology is transforming the office telephone switchboard into a sophisticated minicomputer and the office telephone into a data processing terminal. This dramatic change is coming about after a slow start. Since 1968, when the FCC made the historic Carterfone decision that non-Bell System equipment could be connected to Bell System lines, customers can purchase their office telephone equipment. One major result is an increasing number of new companies and intense competition in the design and manufacture of office switchboards.

When the switchboard, known technically as a **PBX** or **private branch exchange**, was first installed in a customer's office in the 1890s, the telephone company retained ownership of the equipment. The PBX provided a mechanical switching device to replace the earlier hand-operated device located in the telephone company's central office. A **switching device** is needed to control the incoming and outgoing calls to and from a number of telephones. Over the years, the mechanical switching system with its cords and plugboard was replaced by an electromechanical pushbutton model. With the introduction of automatic dialing without operator assistance to telephones outside the office, PBX became **PABX** or **private automatic branch exchange**.

Although AT&T introduced electronic switching systems in its central offices as early as 1965, it took until 1975 to introduce its electronic switchboard, the Dimension PBX.[17] Electromechanical technology in the design of switchboards continued into the 1970s, while computer technology was revolutionizing other office equipment and procedures. A PBX model designed in 1937 was still offered as late as 1971.[18]

The Carterfone decision ended the control over PBX design by the Bell System and its 24 operating companies—a control based on ownership of more than 80 percent of the nation's 200,000 PBXs and more than 90 percent of the nation's 15 million PBX telephones. (Some 1,700 independent telephone companies also depend on the Bell System for equipment.) As a result, many new manufacturers rushed into the market with telephone equipment. The new industry had rough sledding, how-

---

[17] "Technology Changes the Office Telephone," *Business Week* (January 19, 1976).
[18] *Ibid.*

ever, because of Bell's requirement that an **interconnect** device be **added as protection between the privately owned telephone equipment on the customer's premises and the Bell System's telephone lines.** However, the FCC has now ruled that nonBell equipment may be attached without the Bell manufactured interface device.

The telephone monopoly is, however, lobbying with great zeal in the Congress for legislation that would set aside the FCC decisions. The controversy will undoubtedly continue for some time.

Meanwhile, the interconnect companies have boosted their share of total PBX installations to 6 percent and about 1 million PBX telephones, and these figures are expected to double in a few years, according to a Stanford Research Institute economist.[19] Competition from the interconnect companies has resulted in a major effort by the Bell System to replace its obsolete—but highly profitable—PBX installations with new computerized models. During 1975, about 2,500 customer-owned switchboards were installed as interconnected systems, compared with 7,500 installed by the telephone company. Thus the switchboard market is split into 25 percent interconnect companies and 75 percent telephone companies. The new electronic switchboards have made obsolete at least 85 percent of the nation's PBXs, which means a potential market of 170,000 for eventual replacement.[20]

COMPUTERIZED OFFICE SWITCHBOARDS. The new electronic switchboards are made possible by the same low-cost, large-scale integrated circuits (LSI) found in pocket calculators and digital watches. Solid-state computer technology is greatly increasing the versatility and efficiency of the office telephone. Telephone features provided by computer control are impressive. They range from a tone alert to let a caller know that another call is waiting, to automatic forwarding of calls from one extension to another, automatic calling back when an extension is busy, and automatic setting up of conference calls. A telephone can be set up to forward calls to another telephone when a person steps out of the office or takes a coffee break.

The blend of computer and telephone technologies in the new switchboards eliminates the need for physically rewiring a customer's office any time a switchboard is changed, usually an expensive process. The program (or operating instruction) for the switchboard is stored on a tiny silicon chip or microprocessor (discussed earlier in Chapter 7). By changing the program stored in the PBX's computer memory, one can add or eliminate operating features simply. Miniature electronic circuitry makes it economically possible to computerize even small switchboards with only 50 telephones.

---

[19] *Ibid.*
[20] Harry Newton, "The Office Telephone: Today's Most Visible Communications Revolution," *Telephone Engineer & Management* (March 15, 1976), p. 12.

Electronic switchboards handle the management of communications automatically by recording outgoing calls by extension, by placing toll restriction controls on long-distance calls, and by selecting the least expensive route for outgoing calls, which greatly increases the efficiency of line usage. Programming allows incoming messages to be stored for later delivery and office dictation to be recorded on voice store-and-forward magnetic media for later transcription. The stored program switchboards even provide toll accounting and traffic analysis to minimize expenditures and to optimize equipment usage. Whereas a few years ago, an electronic switchboard might have 2,000 words of memory, today it can contain 4,000 words; and some manufacturers of switchboard equipment are examining the possibility of 8,000 words.[21]

TELEPHONE TECHNOLOGY. The earliest PBX technology was based on a **space division** mode of operation, which is still used by most PBX systems today. When a telephone number is dialed in the space division mode, each dial turn activates a switching relay point, and all switch connections remain busy until the user completes the call and hangs up. Then the system tears down all the connections in preparation for the next call. This step-by-step operation requires a huge area for mechanical equipment, and some recent PBX electronic systems that use the best-path method of space division still require large areas of space for the switching mechanisms, which are electromechanical.[22]

The latest PBX technology, using pushbutton phones, is based on a **time division** mode of operation that takes a single path to make a connection. Each conversation has its own time slot along a general pathway. By scanning a single talking path, the time division mode splits it into many different segments of time,[23] a process known technically as **time division multiplexing**. As a result, physical switching mechanisms are no longer necessary.

PBX switchboards all perform a sequence of operations. The sequence is stored either in the machine as part of the hardware or in a program for the machine as software. An electronic PBX, governed by wired logic, has a switching mechanism included as hardware and uses a space division or SD mode of operation; but a PBX governed by software or a programmed memory is considered a stored program machine and uses a time division or TD mode.

Stored programs using the time division mode of operation have made digital switching feasible, thus providing the switchboard with a data processing capability. The Datapax PBX made by Interconnect

---

[21] Joan Zaffarano, "The New Telephones . . . and All Their Smart Switchboards," *Administrative Management* (November 1975), p. 38.
[22] *Ibid.*, p. 40.
[23] *Ibid.*

Resources has sufficient excess storage core in its computer to handle data processing tasks, such as a payroll for 100 employees.[24]

Stored program telephone switchboards are found in the under 100-line category as well as in the upper size range of 1000 lines. AT&T offers the Dimension PBX in two line sizes—40 to 100 lines and 100 to 400 lines. The Dimension, based on **pulse code amplitude**, operates in the time division mode and is the first stored program PBX below 60 lines.[25] Rolm Corporation makes a CBX or Computerized Branch Exchange that accommodates from 100 to 800 lines and 120 trunks. Unlike AT&T's Dimension PBX, the CBX is capable of accepting a microwave transmission hookup and operating at higher line speeds, since its technology is based on **pulse code modulation**, essentially a digital technique. Recently installed at Century Bank & Trust Company in Malden, Massachusetts, the Rolm CBX (shown in Figure 8-3) records outgoing calls by extension and department. **AIOD** or **automatic identification of outward dialing is a process by which phone call data are recorded on paper tape or magnetic tape, from which a computer printout is made for analysis and accounting purposes by the company.**[26] The diagram in Figure 8-4 illustrates the process.

Many new key systems are currently on the market for small firms that require telephone systems of up to 50 stations. The term **key system** refers to **a group of multibutton telephone instruments that provide access to all central office trunk lines as well as intercommunication connections for everyone within a small organization.** Since these systems require no switching equipment, each instrument becomes a switchboard for the entire office. However, multibutton instruments are costly, and an electronic PBX may prove less expensive (depending on the number of telephones needed).

PBX equipment is offered by a number of manufacturers in competition with AT&T. However, the question of interconnecting their equipment with the Bell System is still a major issue, with AT&T facing antitrust suits in the courts. The FCC is concerned over the possibility that AT&T is attempting to drive competitors out of business.[27]

In any event, the latest electronic PBXs based on digital operating techniques are making communications management a close ally of data and word processing. The word **digital** is the important distinction between the new and the old switchboards. When voice signals are converted into digital pulses by the PBX, then all telephone traffic assumes a common format, whether the traffic involves the human voice, the computer signal, the communicating typewriter, or facsimile. All

---

[24] *Ibid.*, p. 35.
[25] *Ibid.*, p. 36.
[26] *Ibid.*, p. 35.
[27] *Ibid.*, p. 42.

Telecommunications

FIGURE 8-3
Answering telephone calls and directing phone traffic at Century Bank and Trust Company of Malden, Massachusetts, have been made more efficient with the installation of a Rolm computerized telephone switching system serving five branch locations.

can be transmitted over a common communications network. The efficient transmission of mixed traffic, whether voice, data, or image, over a single network represents a technological revolution in telecommunications, and digital transmission is AT&T's fastest growing medium.[28] A common communications network is also a vital component of a total management information system.

---

[28] Newton, op. cit., p. 12.

132 Word Processing and Management Information Systems

FIGURE 8-4 AUTOMATIC TELEPHONE SYSTEM

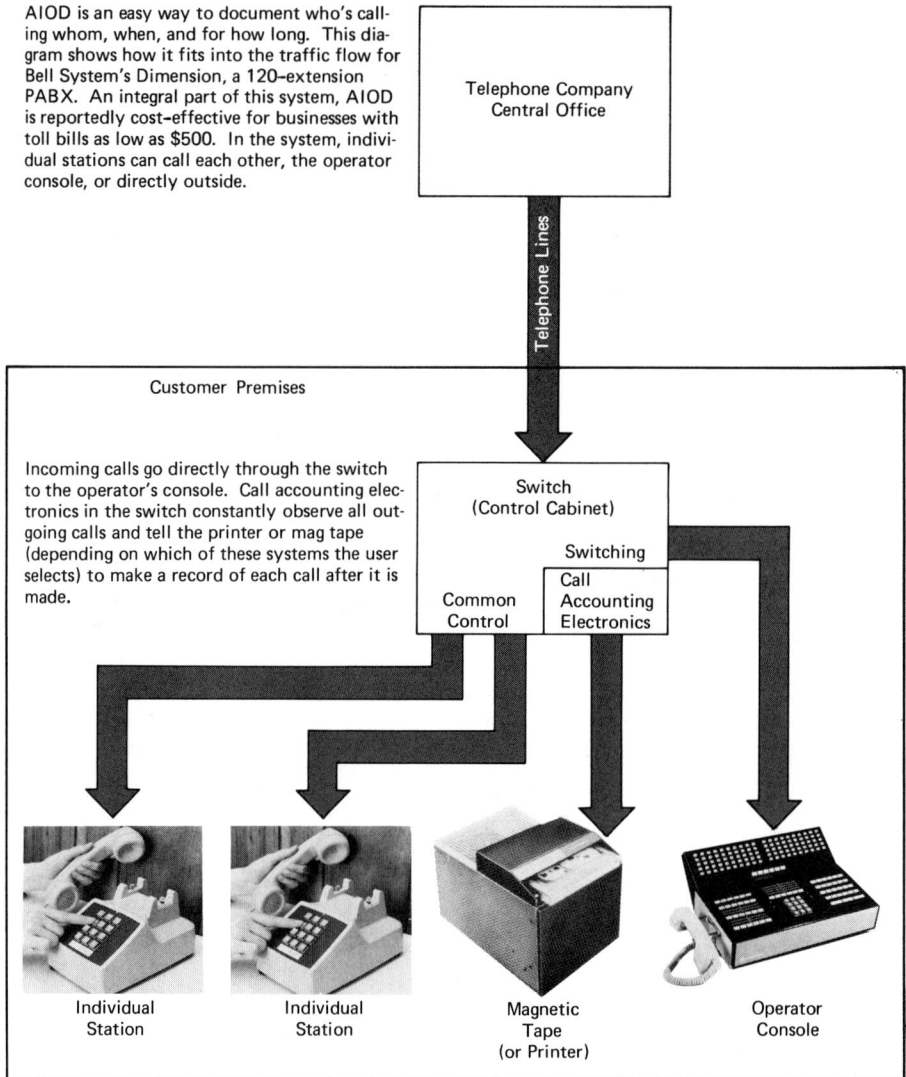

Source: *Administrative Management*, November 1975, p. 36. "The New Telephones . . . And All Their Smart Switchboards," by Joan Zaffarano.

RECORDS MANAGEMENT

The information explosion produced by computers and the resultant flood of paper threaten to engulf white-collar workers. In the attempt to control and organize the tremendous quantities of paper used in office communications, records management is recognized as an integral part of an effective management information system. Records management takes in not only paper records but magnetic media of all types, microfilm systems, and word processing (which is also referred to as **correspondence management**). Particular areas of concern in records management include legal problems of documentation—too much or too little—and regulations concerning the privacy of information.[29]

Businesses are required to keep hundreds of types of records to comply with some 900 regulations issued by nearly sixty bureaus and offices of the federal government. To these must be added the requirements of state and local governments. In the past forty years, correspondence generated by government has increased sixty-fold. Computers and other office machines produce checks, vouchers, purchase orders, payrolls, statements, and tabulations in record numbers. The extent to which a company is government regulated, the scope and complexity of its work, and the efficiency of its management are factors that determine the value of records and the cost of keeping them. On the average, the creation of a four-drawer file for paper documents can cost over $600; and the annual cost of maintaining it, including floor space, supplies, salaries, and overhead, ranges from $250 to $750.[30]

MICROFILM Like computer technology, the trend in record-keeping technology is toward miniaturization. The use of **microfilm,** for instance, can reduce storage space requirements by 98 percent. Microfilm is **a document just as paper is, in that it records permanent, rather than transient, information. The images on microfilm, however, have been reduced to a size that requires an optical magnifying device for reading.** Reduction in size is both an advantage and a disadvantage. The tiny size means that images must be blown back in a larger size on the screen of a reader machine or produced as an enlarged paper print by a reader-printer machine. Microfilm cameras are available that provide variable reduction ratios; reader machines come with interchangeable drop-in and zoom lenses to offer the user a choice of blowbacks (blow-ups); and a variety of reader-printer machines now offer output prints measuring 8½ inches by 11 inches.[31] The three giants of the microfilm industry are the 3M Company, Bell & Howell, and Kodak.

---

[29] "Records Management Goes on Record," *Infosystems* (November 1975), p. 41.
[30] *Ibid.*
[31] Joan Zaffarano, "The Uses of Microfilm," *Administrative Management* (June 1975), p. 44.

The adaptability of microfilm and the need to reduce paper and processing costs make likely the expanding use of microfilm as a dynamic tool in management information systems. In addition to document storage, rapid retrieval, distribution, and **remote access** (which means the ability to make use of documents from a distance), updating and the need to purge (clean out obsolete material) are also required procedures in records management. Microfilm has the potential for meeting all these requirements.

Rapid data retrieval is essential in many operations; otherwise, the data lose their value. With microfilm, a three- to four-second lookup is possible, depending on the **microform** used—**roll or fiche. Roll film** (cartridges and cassettes) can hold up to 3,000 pages, with images stored sequentially along the length of the film. Retrieval, similar to that used with magnetic tape or audio tape records, depends on locating a sequence number on the roll. This procedure is quite different from looking through a paper file. It can prove an obstacle to quick retrieval. **Microfiche** mounted on aperture cards provides discrete units of information. Each card contains up to 98 pages—reduced from an 8½ by 11-inch size. Since a limited number of pages are contained on each card, the fiche file is easily indexed, and the search is made either by machine or by hand. A single compact 16 by 7¾-inch fiche tray holds up

FIGURE 8-5
Various forms of microfilm are shown above—roll film, cartridges and cassettes, as well as microfiche.

FIGURE 8-6
A microfiche reader.

to 500 microfiche cards or a total of 49,000 documents—enough to fill four 4-drawer file cabinets.[32]

In computer terminology, a fiche or aperture card file is a "random access" file. (See Figure 8-6.). Searching for a document in a desktop fiche file is similar to looking through an index card file. The documents are **on-line** or directly accessible to a reader at all times. The high quantity of information stored on microfiche speeds retrieval. The reduction in volume of records with microfiche is astounding. When the City of Los Angeles placed a million engineering drawings on aperture cards, three floors of vaults in the city hall became office space, and one person was able to do the work of ten in storage and retrieval.[33]

Copies of microfilm files are inexpensive to make, once a film master

---

[32] *Ibid.*, p. 46.
[33] "Records Management goes on Record," *op. cit.*, p. 41.

is produced. A million pages duplicated on microfilm might cost roughly $500. Dissemination of duplicate copies of microfilm is also quick and inexpensive because of the reduced size. For example, a multipage microfilm document can be mailed at considerably less postage cost than a similar paper document. When the microfilm document arrives at its destination, paper copies can be printed out in the exact number needed by the recipient. Microfilm duplicators are faster and less costly than photocopiers. A microfilm duplicator costs under $1,500 and copies 200 pages of fiche in fifteen seconds for 5 cents each.[34] Inexpensive copies make it feasible for an executive, for example, to carry the office files along on business trips or when working at home. Fiche cards slip easily into a coat pocket or purse and can be magnified on small pocket-size readers.

Microfilm makes possible complete files that are less likely to be impaired than paper files. Paper documents are more difficult to keep intact and to maintain, since paper is more easily misplaced and less durable for archival use than film. Because of the time needed to inventory and discard paper, purging files in a paper filing system is costly. If outdated microfilm records are retained, little space is lost; consequently, the need to purge is lessened. On the other hand, a mechanized retrieval system with a sensing device can search the densely stored information on microfilm far more quickly than a person can search paper files.

A CASE STUDY OF MACHINE-RETRIEVABLE MICROFILM In 1974, Northwest Region Zellerbach Paper Company, in Portland, Oregon, converted its order-entry files to machine-retrievable microfilm.[35] A Kodak Miracode II encoder, microfilmer, and retrieval terminal was the equipment used, along with a Recordak Prostar film processor. The office serves over 4,000 active customers with over 10,000 items for sale; approximately 500 orders are filled daily. As documents relating to customer orders are received, they are sorted into 100 categories, using as a basis the last two digits of their computer-assigned customer code number. After batching, the documents are reduced 24 times and recorded on 16mm microfilm.

Each 100-foot roll of film takes about 1,700 documents. After a roll is completely exposed, the self-threading Recordak Prostar processes the film. Within ten minutes, the film is ready for the active files. Before filing, the film is spliced into magazines, and each magazine is labeled with the last two digits of the customer code number, as well as the first and last date that information was entered.

---

[34] Zaffarano, "The Uses of Microfilm," op. cit., p. 53.

[35] Maxie S. Day, "Microfilm Retrieval System Provides Savings in Space, Personnel and Supplies," Corporate Systems (June/July 1976).

Records Management

In order to retrieve a file, one places a magazine with the appropriate digit code in the retrieval terminal of the Miracode II. The user then keys in the complete number for that customer, and the machine searches for the latest microfilm entry to the customer's file, displays it on a screen, and produces a full-size paper copy at the push of a button.

With the microfilm system, more than 700 retrievals a day are possible, compared with the previous 200. More importantly, sales representatives find the system an important sales tool and set aside time each week to review the order-entry files of their customers. By reviewing previous purchases, they can pinpoint their sales calls. In addition, the answers to a customer's order-related questions are at their fingertips. Another important benefit is file security. The microfilm magazines containing all the active files are stored in a cabinet that can be rolled into a fireproof vault and locked up at night—quite a contrast to the fifty 4-drawer file cabinets previously needed.

COMPUTER OUTPUT MICROFILM OR COM Computer output microfilm or COM is the combination of two technologies, computers and micrographics. It provides an important solution to problems of modern information systems. **COM can be defined as microfilm that contains data produced from computer-generated signals or as a recording device that converts computer data into readable language directly on microfilm.**[36] COM also refers to the micrographic method used in the system.

Perhaps the simplest way to understand COM is first to think of it as a method and compare it with two other methods used to convert computer data into readable human language—electric typewriters and printers. Whereas electric typewriters and printers produce computer printouts *on paper* from computer tapes, COM recorders produce printouts *on microfilm*. The lightning speed of a COM recorder in printing out computer data can be seen by comparing it with a printer and electric typewriter, as shown below:[37]

	COM	Impact Printer	Electric Typewriter
Characters per Second	80,000	5,000	20
Lines per Minute	36,575	2,275	17
Pages per Hour	34,295	2,135	14

COM has the capability of printing at computer tape speed, with output ten to twenty times greater than that of the electromechanical printers used in standard computer operations.

---

[36] Harold G. Nonemacher, "The Basics of Computer Output Microfilm (COM)," *Management World* (June 1976), p. 24.

[37]*Ibid.*, p. 27.

COM recorders are of two types—on-line and off-line. The on-line device, which is directly attached to the computer unit, operates as a substitute for a high-speed printer. A COM off-line recorder, not wired to a computer system, operates independently, with its own tape drive, and accepts magnetic tape from a computer as input for processing.

Whether on-line or off-line, COM recorders have the same basic components, consisting of input media from the computer, a programming unit, a CRT display, and output from a camera. Some COM units have internal minicomputers for more complex programming capabilities. Information from the computer tapes is displayed on a CRT screen in typewritten format, one line at a time, until a full page of data appears on the screen. Then it is recorded on microfilm by a camera, which is built in to the COM recorder. An on-line COM recorder is used in the Micro 4000 System shown in Figure 8–7. With off-line COM recorders, an outside service organization usually handles the processing of the microfilm and cuts it to standard fiche size.

Both methods, on-line and off-line, have distinct advantages and disadvantages; but the off-line COM unit is generally preferred for several reasons. When the COM unit is off-line, neither the COM recorder nor the computer depend on one another. Independent operations provide greater flexibility and savings in computer time and expense. Computer personnel need not be trained in sophisticated micrographics technology when COM units are separate from the computer. In addition, COM microfiche titling and indexing methods in popular use are best applied with off-line units.[38]

The city of Los Angeles saved thousands of work hours when its animal-licensing-regulation records were converted to COM, and the Los Angeles public library system replaced tons of data processing cards by using COM for checking out books. At present, COM output is used mostly for financial records or other data processing applications, but a trend toward using it for handling personnel records is developing. As a result, the use of COM is expected to spread to other information functions, particularly in banks, insurance companies, and utilities.

A CASE STUDY OF COMPUTER OUTPUT MICROFILM The monumental record-keeping problems of the Illinois Department of Revenue are being solved through the use of Computer Output Microfilm.[39] At the same time, improved service is available to taxpayers. The department collects more than $4 billion in tax revenues annually, maintains files on

---

[38] *Ibid.*, p. 27.

[39] J. Kent Patrick, "The Quicker Answer via COM," *Administrative Management* (June 1976).

Records Management

FIGURE 8-7 THE MICRO 4000

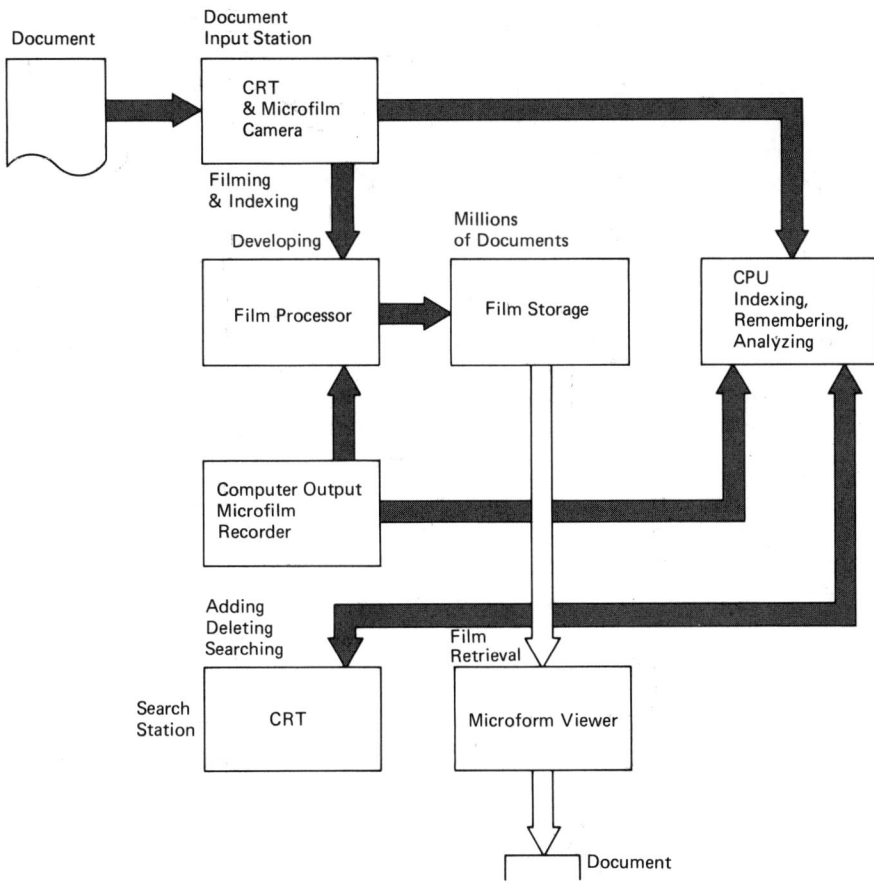

FIGURE 8-7
The Micro 4000 System provides management with control of documents and ease in handling them. A document in the form of paper (hard copy) or in the form of magnetic media is first indexed at the document input station shown in the diagram and microfilmed. Next, the document is stored electronically in the computer while the microfilm version is processed and then stored in a central file or film storage. The central file index may consist of a key word or key information used to locate the filed document, either in the computer or in the film storage. The file index is accessible from any CRT search station within the system. Once the filed document is located, it can either be viewed on the CRT video screen or the microfilm version can be seen on a microform viewer. If required, a paper copy of the document can then be produced.

Source: Lawrence W. Harrod, Charter Member of the Federal Government Micrographics Council.

over 10 million forms and associated tax documents, pays out about $200 million in tax refunds or tax relief grants to some 3 million taxpayers, and keeps over 100 million computer file records to control the whole process. Perhaps the most difficult task to handle, however, is the more than 500,000 inquiries received annually from taxpayers—half of these in the form of telephone calls to Taxpayers' Service Units in Springfield and Chicago.

COM permits the effective and rapid retrieval of information stored in computer files in order to respond to this flood of inquiries. Details of an individual's tax record are provided by COM without expensive on-line inquiry into the computer data-based files and without the costly, time-consuming bulkiness of handling paper documents.

The department reduces vital taxpayer information stored in computer files to 16mm COM cartridges. The process makes possible an immediate response by the service clerk to telephone inquiries from Illinois taxpayers. The equipment used is a 3M series F COM unit, consisting of a magnetic tape drive, controller, electron beam recorder, and an image recorder. The unit produces on microfilm from computer tapes all the taxpayers' account ledgers. Duplication is handled by a Canon 800 H duplicator capable of processing 200 feet of film a minute. Also included in the system are 34 3M series 500 reader/printers. By utilizing account ledgers, which are produced on microfilm at regular intervals and contain all the pertinent data entered into the computer files, the COM unit permits service clerks to respond to inquiries in minutes. There is seldom a need for delay or for a follow-up letter or phone call. This is in sharp contrast to the previously estimated transaction time of anywhere from eight hours to three weeks.

PHOTOCOPIERS Records management is concerned not only with the indexing, storing and retrieval of documents, but with correspondence management or word processing. Once the office word processing system produces a document, records management becomes involved in methods of copying the document for distribution, a related but separate operation. Dozens of models of photocopy machines are marketed by many different companies. Some of the firms marketing plain paper copiers are Xerox, IBM, Dennison, Royal, AM, Savin, Van Dyke, Remington, Pitney Bowes, Kodak, SCM, and A.B. Dick. The number of machines available makes the process of selecting and managing copy equipment a complex one. Significant features, apart from the quality of the copy, include speed and cost per copy, as well as ability to meet an organization's specific needs, which may include collating, duplexing, and reduction capabilities.

A company that requires a single copy of an original document needs a different type of copier from that needed by a company that requires multiple copies of multipage, outsized documents. Some of the newer machines, for example the IBM Series III Copier/Duplicator, feature an advanced document feed that automatically positions the original document and produces the first copy in 4.5 seconds and subsequent copies every $^8/_{10}$ of a second, or 75 per minute. **Duplexing** permits both sides of a document page to be copied. From 1 to 999 copies can be made automatically, and a document of up to 100 pages can be collated with this type of machine. Two reduction modes are possible—26 percent or 35 percent; and original documents up to 12 by 17 inches are accepted by the machine, including 11 by 14 inch computer printouts. Needless to say, the amount of paper required to operate these machines is enormous.

PHOTOTYPESETTING Another operation related to records management and integral to word processing is typesetting. Whether typewritten documents are duplicated, copied, or printed, converting processed words into typeset words is an advantage, since the space required is 40 percent less than that needed for typewritten words.[40] As a result, costs of mail, distribution, paper, and labor are also less. Another advantage is that typographic copy provides bold headings, italics, and other niceties that improve the readability of documents.

Word processing technology makes typesetting and composition relatively simple compared with older typesetting methods. The word processing secretary's original keystrokes on an automatic typewriter are recorded on magnetic media. The media are then used as direct input to a phototypesetter or into video terminals of a computer-controlled typesetter. Any additional changes are then made, and command codes for type size, style, and format are inserted.[41] Since 60 percent of the cost of typesetting comes from rekeyboarding of copy, proofreading, and correcting the errors made during rekeyboarding, printshop costs are substantially reduced by using the original, error-free recorded keystrokes made by the word processing secretary.[42]

At present, only about one third of the nationwide 16,460 medium and large corporate printshops (those with more than five in-house employees) have integrated their printing equipment with the office word processing system. However, 80 percent of them are expected to make the connection soon. Apart from newspapers, magazines, and books, more than 50 percent of all printed pages in the U.S. are produced at in-plant locations, usually in large companies. Big savings are possible for

---

[40] "WP: Path to the 80s," *Modern Office Procedures* (June 1975), p. 98.

[41] *Ibid.*

[42] "The New Technology Spurs Corporate Printers," *Business Week* (June 30, 1975), p. 64.

companies willing to invest at least $6,000 to $12,000 for a fully integrated system linking the word processing center with the printshop. Trans World Airlines, Inc., made the tie starting in 1969 and now has 28 administrative manuals, including accounting, personnel, and communications procedures, on 5,000 tapes. By using word processing to prepare hard copy for phototypesetting in the TWA printshop, TWA estimates a saving of at least $300,000 per year.[43]

EXECUTIVE CONTROL AND ORGANIZATIONAL STRUCTURES

Computers have been disrupting traditional office organization ever since data processing was first introduced into the bookkeeping and accounting areas. The combination of computer technology with other office technologies, such as word processing, telecommunications, and records management, is causing further drastic changes in procedures within large organizations, changes designed to improve operating efficiency and to increase profits. Unless these changes are controlled and directed by management, organizations cannot survive and continue to grow. The function of management is to lead, to make decisions, and to give direction to an enterprise.

Management tends to overlook its potential for executive control by placing the four areas of word processing, data processing, telecommunications, and records management under the general supervision of an administrative officer in the organization. Administration is usually regarded as a separate department that provides support services for other corporate departments. Considering the importance of these four areas in day-to-day operations, management does well to give them not only continuing support but also recognition as separate subsystems of management itself.

One means of creating a management information system and opportunities for automating the executive control function is to integrate the word processing, data processing, records management, and telecommunications segments under a company officer responsible for information services rather than administration. Information flow in a company must travel not only from the top down but from the subsystems up to top management, and across subsystems as well. This is necessary if cost-effective operations are to be established. The vast amount of new equipment and alternative services available in the marketplace requires careful cost-performance analysis if these four developing areas are to become manageable resources. Certainly, when a company spends millions of dollars a year on communications, information services becomes a full-time function. Administrative or financial personnel

---

[43] *Ibid.*

FIGURE 8-8 INFORMATION SERVICES

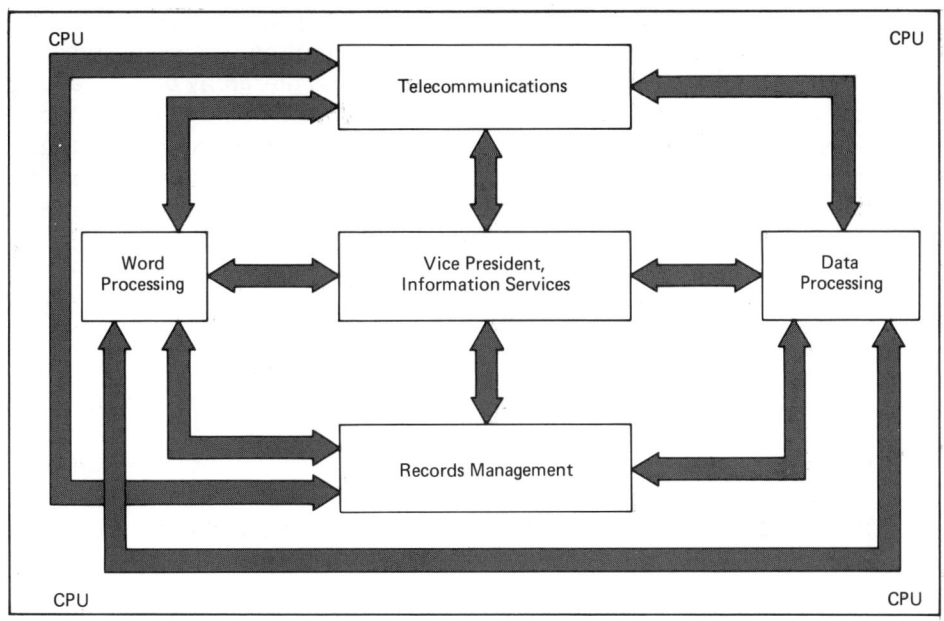

Manager, Word Processing System	Manager, Records Management	Manager, Telecommunications	Manager, Data Processing

Secretarial Services
  Dictation
  Word Processing
  Administrative
  Support
 	
Stationery and
  Supplies
 	
Mail and Messengers
	Storage and Retrieval
	
	Corporate Records
	
	Microfilm and COM
	
	Photocopiers
	
	Phototypesetting
		Switchboard and Telephones
		
		Transmission Networks
		
		Electronic Mail
		
		Facsimile
		
		TWX/Telex
		
		Mailgrams
			Accounting
			
			Payroll
			
			Personnel Records
			
			Financial Reports
			
			Inventory of Office Equipment

are not equipped, as a rule, to handle the technical nature of these areas. Personnel with professional expertise, who understand the options and equipment and who have the ability to manage and control costs, are needed to manage each of the four information subsystems in a large organization.

The incredible speed of computer technology, which permits processing enormous amounts of information, requires a corresponding speed in decision-making and delegation of authority over broad areas of operations. Decisions must be made at the operational level by experts in the field. These decisions must be known by management, however, if executive control and overall organizational policies are to be maintained. Computer technology is, therefore, creating increasing pressure on traditional organization structures. The rigid hierarchy of the mechanical industrial era is expected to give way to a flexible structure that is better adapted to the electronic era of instant communication. If management is to exercise executive control, one-way communication from the top down must change to two-way communication between management and personnel at every organizational level.

One management solution for achieving two-way communications within a large organization is a flexible network structure. A network resembles the web of a spider. The spider sits in the center and senses immediately when something enters its surrounding web. A web or network woven of wires connecting the central processing unit of a central office computer to terminals in the various offices of an organization can place management in the center of the communication flow. The physical location of the personnel involved is of little consequence, as long as they are linked to management through the computer network.

If the computer network is seen as a "field" in which the various operations of the organization take place, then everyone working for that organization is operating within a common field. Communication flows within that common field. The network structure provides for the flow of information to all of the organization's subsystems operating within the field. A diagram of this type of network operating within a common computer field is shown in Figure 8–8, together with one suggested way of organizing the four subsystems of an information services network. Information can flow from the center out to the subsystems and from the subsystems to the center, as well as among the subsystems themselves, thus providing a flow of information to all parts of the system.

Connections currently being made to a computer central processing unit, including the equipment and procedures discussed in this chapter, are illustrated in Figure 8–9. These include the connections made through a company computer-based switchboard (PABX) for dictation and data processing, and the direct connection to the computer central processing unit for other word processing and records management functions. A recent study by Quantum Science Corporation indicates that the computer-based switchboard will also bridge the various administrative office functions to security and control systems as well as linking these systems to the data processing center.[44]

---

[44] Edward K. Yasaki, "Toward the Automated Office," *Datamation* (February 1975), p. 61.

Executive Control and Organizational Structures 145

FIGURE 8-9 THE AUTOMATED OFFICE OF THE FUTURE

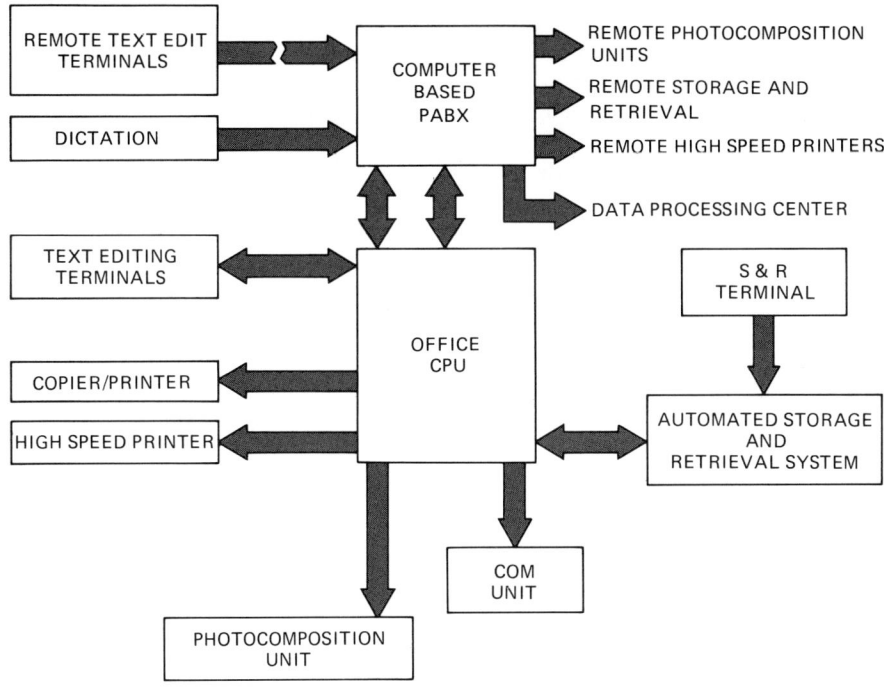

FIGURE 8-9
Text editing, document preparation, facsimile transmission, automated file systems, and programmable switchboards exist separately today. Integrated, they could make up the automated office of the future.

Reprinted with permission of Datamation®, © 1975 by Technical Publishing Company, Greenwich, Conn.

A multimedia environment of information handling with executive control is possible, using a flexible network structure within an organization; but the decision to move toward a network structure is up to management. The building blocks for the automated office of the future are clearly discernible in the technology now available. It remains only for executives to develop creative, new, and imaginative procedures to tap the tremendous potential of electronic technology and to achieve a total management information system. This future, the paperless, automated office visible on the contemporary scene, will be discussed in the final chapter.

SUGGESTED READINGS

BYLINSKY, GENE. "Datran's Hazardous High-Wire Act," *Fortune*, February 1976, pp. 131–139.

DAY, MAXIE S. "Microfilm Retrieval System Provides Savings in Space, Personnel and Supplies," *Corporate Systems*, June/July 1976, pp. 49, 54, 56.

"Facsimile Usage to Pick Up Steam in Next Two Years," *Infosystems*, September 1975, p. 33.

FORD, KENNETH W. "The Management of Information," *The Office*, September 1974, pp. 18–20.

"Micrographics Gains Recognition as a Dynamic Systems Tool," *Infosystems*, September 1975, pp. 21–22.

MITCHELL, JOHN W. "New Direction for WP: The Communications Management Department," *Word Processing Report*, Vol. 8, No. 11, June 1, 1975.

"The New Technology Spurs Corporate Printers," *Business Week*, June 30, 1975, p. 64.

NEWTON, HARRY. "The Office Telephone: Today's Most Visible Communications Revolution," *Telephone Engineer & Management*, March 15, 1976, pp. 12–14.

NONEMACHER, HAROLD G. "The Basics of Computer Output Microfilm (COM)," *Management World* (June 1976), 24–28.

"The Office of the Future," *Business Week*, June 30, 1975, pp. 48–84.

PATRICK, J. KENT. "The Quicker Answer via COM," *Administrative Management*, June 1976, pp. 40–48.

"Records Management Goes on Record," *Infosystems*, Vol. 22, No. 11, November 1975, pp. 41–42.

TAPPY, T. P. "Taming the Paperwork Explosion," *Management World*, July 1976, pp. 3–5.

"Technology Changes the Office Telephone," *Business Week*, January 19, 1976.

THOMAS, RONALD R. "Corporate Telecommunications—A Manageable Resource," *Management World*, Vol. 5, No. 4, April 1976, pp. 11–13.

———. "Your Private Branch Exchange (PBX)," *Management World*, June 1976, pp. 10–11.

"Washington Innovates to Cope with Paperwork," *Business Week*, June 30, 1975, p. 50.

"WP: Path to the 80s," *Modern Office Procedures*, Vol. 20, No. 6, June 1975, pp. 93–99.

YASAKI, EDWARD K. "Toward the Automated Office," *Datamation*, February 1975, pp. 59–62.

ZAFFARANO, JOAN. "The Uses of Microfilm," *Administrative Management*, Vol. XXXVI, No. 6, June 1975, pp. 36–54.

———. "The New Telephones . . . and All Their Smart Switchboards," *Administrative Management*, Vol. XXXVII, No. 11, November 1975, pp. 35–44.

Chapter

THE AUTOMATED PAPERLESS OFFICE OF THE FUTURE

Words written on paper are a primary part of office communication, and, for that reason, modern word processing (or automation in the production of written words) is viewed as an opening wedge toward revolutionizing office work. By speeding paperwork production, however, word processing has so far only increased the flood of paper that threatens to overwhelm office workers. Over $40 billion was spent in 1974 alone in paperwork required for governmental agencies. Add to that the amount of nongovernmental paperwork, and the cost staggers the imagination. The solution to the paper problem anticipated by many experts is that electronic record-handling will gain acceptance; and, before the end of the century, offices will become almost paperless. A decline in the use of paper in office communications should be noted during the 1980s. By the 1990s, most office records and correspondence will be transmitted, viewed, and stored on electronic media. Even now, the widespread use of magnetic media in office systems technology seems to support the vision of a paperless office—with one major exception.

Written words are imprinted images. They represent a traditional technology human beings have been using since the invention of writing. Written words stored on magnetic media and viewed on electronic video terminals represent a highly complex, different technology. The written message is first encoded in digital format then decoded into words. Replacing written words on paper with magnetic media projections on electronic screens will require office workers not simply to learn new ways but to "unlearn" old ways. Electronic words also require changes in basic office equipment and work procedures. Changes in office equipment in turn require changes in organization and personnel. A sizeable segment of the people who will work in offices in the 1990s are teenagers and college students today. Therefore, consideration of the changes electronic technology will have on these basic ingredients —office equipment and procedures, organizational structure, and office workers—is needed in order to hazard a guess about the automated office of the future. Since office systems are also subsystems of a larger environment, the American social scene toward the end of the twentieth century is another relevant factor. First consideration, however, is of office workers, the most essential element in offices of the 1990s.

OFFICE WORKERS OF THE 1990s

In large measure, the work force of the 1990s will be made up of today's high school and college students. Approximately 30 percent of them will have earned a four-year college degree or something higher. These higher-education attainments mean that American society in the next twenty years will have a younger, well-educated work force replacing an older, less-educated one.[1] Higher education tends to inflate the employment expectations of younger workers, most of whom believe that a good education entitles them to a good job. Women, who have nearly the same education qualifications as men and who have been conspicuously underemployed, will want and, increasingly, expect good jobs on an equal basis with men. By 1990, women are expected to make up over 40 percent of the work force. In round numbers, the civilian work force (all persons sixteen years and over) is expected to climb from 93.5 million in 1975 to over 110 million in 1990. More than half of the nation's workers are expected to be in white-collar jobs.

The young women and men who will make up the largest segment of the future work force share a work ethic considerably different from that of their elders. Surveys indicate sharp differences between generations

---

[1] James O'Toole, "The Reserve Army of the Underemployed," *Change* (May 1975), p. 30.

of values and attitudes toward work. Beginning workers today want jobs that offer challenge, growth, and self-fulfillment. To young people reared in an affluent society, jobs are considered attractive not merely in terms of money or status—these things are more or less taken for granted—but also in terms of interest and meaning. Quality of life is a goal rather than quantity of material things. An Office of Education study of high school seniors shows that when choosing a career, their first preference is for work that is helpful to others and useful to society. Only 18 percent chose "having lots of money" as a primary factor in their lives.[2]

Many of these students have already been introduced to computers, since computer terminals are invading the classroom. In 1975, the National Science Foundation found that nearly 27 percent of the nation's secondary schools already offer some kind of education by computer. As the cost decreases, lessons by computer are expected to increase. A majority of the nation's colleges also offer individualized, give-and-take computer instruction that students study at their own pace. Operating a terminal keyboard, the student carries on a dialogue with the machine while performing a set of programmed exercises. Students of all ages seem to find computer learning effective and a great way to study.[3] Future office workers, who are taught their math in school by conversations with a friendly machine (one that addresses them by name, answers their questions with infinite patience, and includes games or bits of humor in its lessons) are not likely to find computers dehumanizing in the world of work.

OFFICE WORKERS AND COMPUTERS

Specialization in the behavior of living organisms has always been a first step on the road to extinction. As anthropologists and biologists have demonstrated, all human societies and biological species now known to be extinct died out as the result of overspecialization.[4] Humankind as a species is distinguished by its lack of specialization and its unique ability to adapt, characteristics that have made human life possible in the world's varied ecological environments. The mental ability to invent and the physical dexterity to transform ideas into tools are generalized attributes of our species. People are being challenged by computers to relinquish specialization in work tasks and to return to their capability

---

[2] *Ibid.*, p. 31.
[3] Evan Jenkins, "Classroom Revolution: Computer Interaction," *New York Times*, June 13, 1976, Sec. 4, p. 9.
[4] R. Buckminster Fuller, *Operating Manual for Spaceship Earth*. New York: 1969, p. 39.

for wide mental understanding.[5] As the computer's potential becomes fully realized in office management systems, automation will displace routine clerical and other overspecialized positions.

Although the introduction of computers and automation into office work means an end to some special kinds of learning, it is not an end to learning. Automation is also information, and the future of work consists of earning a living in the automation age.[6] Computers are the most powerful tool human beings have yet invented; they extend the limits of the human brain even beyond human comprehension. When considering the capabilities of computers and the human brain, however, it is necessary to distinguish between the human brain and the human mind. The brain is concerned with memory, with specific individual experiences and objective observations; the mind extracts and applies generalized principles and integrates them for effective use.[7] Computers supplement the human brain in calculating, manipulating, and comparing, but not the human mind.

Computers lack judgment and common sense and are naive, following instructions to the letter. In the computer-human being partnership, human beings remain the dominant partner. Control is ensured by the human mind's ability to discern patterns, to know by insight, to create, and to discover. Although our memory stores incredible amounts of information, exceeding the capacity of the computer, it is slow in retrieving information; while the computer retrieves data instantly. With instantaneous speed, electronic computers effortlessly perform calculating and retrieval tasks that were formerly done mechanically and with much time and effort. In the process, computers make new work patterns necessary.

Machines have been replacing workers ever since Americans began the process of technical development and industrialization. In 1876, one of the great international exhibitions was held in Philadelphia. In describing the event, a German reporter, F. Goldschmidt, gave the reasons why Americans were outstripping Europeans in technology. The effort to replace human power by the machine, education directed toward practical ends, extensive division of labor, and a sound patent law were the factors responsible.[8]

Americans are still replacing human power with machines—highly complex electronic computers. Unlike mechanical devices, computers are programmed to perform a variety of tasks, and, simply by a change of program, can be adapted to perform new tasks. The division of labor

---

[5] *Ibid.*, p. 44.

[6] Marshall McLuhan, *Understanding Media*. New York: 1964, p. 346.

[7] Fuller, *op. cit.*, p. 94.

[8] Friedrich Klemm, *A History of Western Technology*. Cambridge, MA: 1964, pp. 328–330.

required by mechanical operations is replaced by a machine that performs every work task. Human power is replaced by electric power. Although power or energy is separate from information, the electronic age of automation tends to fuse power with information, so that production, consumption, and learning become blended in a single process.[9]

Far from needing only an education directed toward practical ends, workers in the new electronic age also need the kind of adaptive skills provided by a liberal education—skills in human communication and social integration. Skills in learning, to absorb new ideas and to discard outmoded ones; skills in relating, to make and maintain human relationships in a mobile society; and skills in choosing, to handle many types of complex situations and decisions—these are the skills needed by workers in the electronic age.[10]

FUTURE OFFICE EQUIPMENT

Equipment in the office of the future is probably the simplest element to predict, because of current trends. The technology is already in existence; only further development is required to automate office work to the extent deemed economically profitable or socially desirable. Since the underlying goal of automation is the reduction of office costs and increased efficiency by using machines in place of people, the office of the future will be equipped with more sophisticated machinery and staffed by considerably fewer people. Even the office messenger's job will be taken over by robot mailmobiles capable of carrying up to 500 pounds of mail, paper supplies, or whatever. The mailmobile is already following invisible chemical guidepaths through offices, announcing its coming with a beep-beep, and carrying messages and paperwork in its travels.[11]

Current trends indicate that stand-alone, single-purpose machines will become multipurpose, integrated office systems. Automatic typewriters, for example, are now capable of communicating with each other, with computers, and with TWX and Telex equipment. Links to computers provide typewriters with access to stored data and information bases, such as prerecorded paragraphs or letters, lists of names and addresses, and also accounts receivable and payable. Before too long, a dictation transcriber will be made an integral part of the typewriter. Ultimately, typewriters will be programmed to turn out finished documents directly from the dictation on magnetic media, with no need for keyboarding by a typist!

Copier machines will be integrated with text-editing typewriters, with

---

[9] McLuhan, op. cit., p. 350.
[10] Alvin Toffler, Future Shock. New York: 1970, pp. 413–418.
[11] "Mail Call Just Won't Be the Same," The New York Times, May 30, 1976.

facsimile, and with microfilming, so that duplicate paper copies can be made automatically by all three. Storage and retrieval systems will be tied closely to a shared processor text-editing typewriter for the indexing and referencing of material at the time original text is keyboarded into the computer.

Further expansion of digital transmission networks and the wider use of computer-based switchboards will link the various functions within offices as well as provide links to systems outside the office. Incoming telephone messages will be stored for later delivery, and incoming calls for dictation will be recorded on voice store-and-forward units for later transcription. A programmable office switchboard will perform certain data processing functions in connection with long distance charges and traffic analysis of telephone calls for the most efficient use of telephone lines. Electronic mail will be widespread. It will be transmitted either directly among private firms over nationwide digital transmission networks or as Mailgrams, by a combination of private and public services.

The trend toward smaller, multipurpose equipment will make computer terminals as commonplace as telephones and radios. The traveling businessperson will carry a portable terminal that needs only a standard pushbutton telephone and an electrical outlet to plug in to direct communication with a home-office computer. Critical sales orders can be confirmed on the spot, or key business information can be exchanged. Texas Instruments, Inc., presently makes a portable model computer terminal that looks like a typewriter, weighs 13 pounds, costs about $2,000, and is quiet enough to use anywhere—in an office, a conference room, or at home.

Television screens and pushbutton phones already have the capability to act as connecting links for distant computers. A future office executive may either work at home at a terminal linked to the office computer or have a small minicomputer for home use. IBM recently introduced a 50-pound computer, the 5100 Portable. Scarcely larger than an office typewriter, the price range of this desk-top computer is comparable to that of an automatic typewriter. Plugs can connect the computer to printers, to telephone lines, or to ordinary television sets for displays useful in group meetings or educational programs. A radical new thing about the portable computer is the fact that it works in **Basic, an easily learned layman's language** that eliminates the need for **Fortran** or **Cobol, the special programming languages used for computers.**

In fact, an increasing amount of office work may be done at home. Recent research and development in telecommunications wiring with optical glass fiber promise hundreds of television channels and two-way communication awaiting future workers. Imagine sitting in front of a home television screen that is capable of letting you carry on a dialogue not only with a distant computer but with a human being. A company executive at home will be able to speak to a secretary at the office while each appears on the other's screen. Business meetings can use split-screen arrangements for conference calls so that people in widely scattered locations, even on different continents, can conduct face-to-face discussions. Long distances lose meaning when satellites are involved in transmitting television programs or data or information, since 3,000 miles involve no greater effort than 300. With future two-way video telephone calls in color, charges will probably not be based primarily on distance.[12]

FUTURE OFFICE PROCEDURES

Future office procedures will change radically as a result of desk-top television screens and computer terminals. Research and development of future office systems by IBM and Xerox indicate two different views of office procedures, based primarily on the different business strategies of each company. Xerox' strength lies in providing the basic building blocks, or machines that perform the most common office functions, with the exception of computers. Xerox pulled out of the computer industry in 1975 and currently believes in decentralizing office processes.[13] The chief research scientist at Xerox says that the office information system will not be a mammoth system for a whole division, plant, or company, but will focus on a manager and a department. What Xerox envisions is a **distributed processing** approach to the office of the future. An important new trend in data processing, distributed processing is a decentralized approach to office systems based on a communications network of minicomputers and remote terminals. These small data processors handle small problems on their own, or they perform the work of a large central computer by teaming up to handle large problems. Xerox plans to develop minicomputer processors, terminals, and an information storage-and-retrieval system that will be adaptable, easy-to-use, "friendly" machines.[14]

IBM, which has its strength in big computers, dominates the computer market. At present, IBM also accounts for almost 90 percent of the market in word processing equipment. IBM is setting the pace in computers and word processing and intends to continue doing so in the automated office of the future. The marketing director of IBM word processing systems indicates that managers are not likely themselves to operate computers. IBM's approach is to use its big central computer systems by placing terminals on the secretary's desk and providing a minimum of hardware in the executive's office.[15]

Since audio devices such as telephones and dictation equipment are

---

[12] Erik Barnouw, "So You Think TV Is Hot Stuff? Just You Wait," *Smithsonian* (July 1976), p. 80.
[13] "The Office of the Future," *Business Week* (June 30, 1975), p. 72.
[14] *Ibid.*
[15] *Ibid.*, p. 84.

the types of machines executives use, IBM developed an experimental system that connects the executive's pushbutton phone to a central computer and to a secretarial station for dictation. The phone can be used as a calculator and to make calls automatically at a preselected time; it also has a six- or eight-line display screen for use in querying a reference library. This concept is based on IBM's private automatic branch exchange, an electronic switchboard that is now marketed in Europe but, because of regulatory and legal questions, is several years away from entry into the U.S. market.[16] While office executives are using the audio devices, secretaries will become computer operators, inputting lengthy documents on the terminal keyboard and retrieving stored material as needed. A part of this concept is IBM's **work-group** approach. A work-group is **a group of company executives with their own word processing center for heavy typing tasks and with administrative secretaries who retain typewriters for light typing.** Both word processing and administrative secretaries will also operate computer terminals. As computer terminals are used more and more for both word processing and data processing applications, the integrated office system will begin to look increasingly like an electronic data processing system.

One large New York law firm that made the commitment to computers in 1969, starting with data processing, recently upgraded the firm's IBM 370 computer in order to increase the number of terminals to thirty. All but two of the terminals are now dedicated to word processing applications. Secretaries in the firm are trained to operate the computer terminals and to work in groups of five secretaries and eight lawyers. As the information base in the computer expands, lawyers in the firm are expected to originate increasing numbers of their documents from preformulated paragraphs and other stored material. The firm uses a modified version of Administrative Terminal System. **ATS is the IBM software package that programs computers for word processing.** It has devised its own instruction manual in nontechnical terminology for training secretaries in computer operations.

If computer word processing is to lead to the management information system that data processing has promised but never delivered, computer terminals will have to become easier to operate. The difficulty with the data processing display terminals used to communicate with computers is that people are forced to learn a computer language and to adapt their work habits to suit the computer. For the past three years, Xerox has been developing an office terminal that substitutes "people culture" for "computer culture." These experimental terminals work informally and require no new human work habits. The terminals call up and display information from an electronic file with incredible speed.

---

[16] *Ibid.*

Future Office Procedures

The terminal user can change the wording of a page displayed on the terminal screen by means of a hand-held, movable control device. Movements of the control device produce similar movements in an electronic pointer on the screen. When the pointer is moved to a word or paragraph to be changed, the user pushes a button marked "cut" and the word or paragraph disappears. Another button marked "paste" provides for insertions in the text at the spot indicated by the pointer.[17]

Also displayed on the terminal screen is an "in-basket" heading. By moving the electronic pointer to the heading, a list of memos and letters that arrived from other office terminals is displayed. If the user wants to read a particular item, the pointer can produce the complete text on the screen. After that, the letter or memo can either be sent to an electronic filing cabinet, or a paper copy can be produced on a printer or copier for the user to retain.[18] Xerox expects both managers and secretaries to use the same terminal. The TV-like display screen is much easier and faster to learn than typewriter word processors. Using the terminals may also produce a long-range tendency for managers to do their own typing and filing. As the cost of electronic circuitry continues to spiral downward, Xerox plans to build a commercial version of this system.

Many business executives already are operating computer terminals in their own offices through the use of outside information services. Some two dozen of these specialized services offer large central memory banks of computers for data ranging from Dow Jones stock-market reports to general news and legal decisions. Abstracts of news stories, stock prices, mergers, and acquisitions are called up on a display screen by punching a key on a computer terminal leased from one of these services. The *New York Times* information bank has a data base starting from its 1969 editions to the present, and from sixty other publications. A typical client might run 150 searches a month on an office video terminal and use a printer for paper copies at a cost of $15,000 or more each year. Lawyers and accountants obtain instant displays of court rulings and government regulations on Lexis terminals leased from Mead Data Central. Lexis can provide information in minutes that might take a lawyer hours to find in a library. However, many customers of these information services find them difficult to use because of the skill needed in asking the right questions of the computer. Experts agree that, as "friendly" terminals become available for these data-base systems and as costs decrease, outside central information banks, capable of being accessed immediately on a computer terminal in the user's office, will become standard office equipment.[19] As office automation

---

[17] *Ibid.*, p. 82.
[18] *Ibid.*
[19] "Selling Data to the Office of the Future," *Business Week* (June 30, 1975), p. 84.

continues to evolve, both office executives and their secretaries are faced with learning to operate many more complex office appliances rather than fewer—not unlike the learning required of American homemakers in operating sophisticated home and kitchen appliances.

FORCES AFFECTING ORGANIZATIONAL STRUCTURES

Despite the business strategies of IBM and Xerox, future organizational structures are not likely to develop solely as a result of new office equipment and work methods. In addition to technology, two other forces are involved in organizational changes: the scale of private enterprise and the environment. Big American corporations continue to get bigger. As they grow, their operations extend geographically to other countries and become the concern of government. The oil companies and the automotive industry are two examples of the international scope of private enterprise. With the growth of large national and multinational corporations and organizations, business becomes increasingly entangled with complex social problems. Efforts to control industrial pollution of the earth's surface, including the oceans and other waterways, and to control the world's population explosion are also matters of grave concern among all peoples of the world. As a result, protection of the environment and conservation of natural resources will be a major force affecting economic growth and development during the next decades.

Every capitalist country today has a growing core of economic planning.[20] In some countries the core is more formalized than in others. In America, economic planning at present is piecemeal and inadequate. Periods of prosperity and full employment alternate with periods of recession and high unemployment. Social Security, unemployment compensation, Medicare, and welfare are all government-sponsored programs that are planned to provide economic benefits not derived spontaneously from the market system.[21] The Federal Reserve Board attempts indirectly to control inflation and plan the economic process, as do wage and price controls enacted during inflationary periods. The need for coordinated planning is amply demonstrated by the lack of knowledge many Americans have about their economy.

During the Arab oil embargo, vital information regarding the amount of gasoline on hand was not available. The inadequacy of unemployment statistics is generally recognized, and little is known about the

---

[20] Robert L. Heilbroner, "The American Plan," *The New York Times Magazine* (January 25, 1976), p. 40.
[21] *Ibid.*, p. 35.

actual numbers or kinds of job openings that exist in the U.S. economy. Yet these are some of the essential facts required in order to make projections and plans for the future and to avoid continuing cycles of unemployment, inflation, and economic waste.

The need for adequate economic planning to overcome the complexities and sheer size of the problems facing the nation is recognized by the Congress. Legislation establishing some form of economic planning board, probably within the President's office, is simply a matter of time. Government officials and representatives from business, labor, and other sectors of the economy, serving on such a board, would then be responsible for drawing up plans for the country's economic growth. Along with this prospect, the influence of government in the economic sphere is having an increasingly important effect on the internal processes and organizational structures of private enterprise.

TWO-WAY COMMUNICATION BETWEEN MANAGEMENT AND EMPLOYEES

One strong indication of the growing influence of government is the recent obligation for effective communication with employees imposed on company management by ERISA, the Employee Retirement Income Security Act of 1974. The law applies to all companies and employee organizations whose welfare benefit plans cover more than 100 participants. Welfare benefit plans include health and hospital insurance as well as pension and profit sharing. The law was passed as the result of abuses by certain companies and labor unions in the handling of pension funds and in depriving workers of their retirement benefits.

ERISA requires that participating companies and organizations disclose to workers covered by a plan full information concerning the benefits offered, written in language simple enough to be understood by the average person. The disclosure requirement applies to almost every company with an employee benefit program and places tremendous responsibility on corporate management in particular.

As a rule, corporate management spends millions of dollars on advertising and public relations to communicate a favorable picture of their companies to customers, investors, and the general public. Although lip service is paid to employee communication in the form of house organs and pamphlets describing employee benefits, management on the whole has done little to establish real communication with employees. Instead, communication is usually limited to telling employees what management wants them to know.[22] The term "human resources" re-

---

[22] Richard W. Darrow, "Employee Communications—Neglected Need," *The New York Times* (December 28, 1975), Sec. 3.

veals management's view of employees as a kind of capital—not as individuals with interests, needs, and wants of their own.

ERISA, on the other hand, requires management to tell employees what they want to know about the company's operations and in language they can understand, thus opening the possibility of two-way communication between employees and management. The ERISA reports, combined with annual operating reports oriented toward employees, can help employees to understand the company and its operations, as well as the economic system that makes their benefits possible.[23] The increasingly higher educational attainments of office workers enable them to understand profit and loss statements, marketing procedures, annual earnings, and dividends to stockholders, when these are clearly presented. Knowledge of a company's operations gives employees a sense of participation. It also results in an informed group of workers, able to assess the company's social role in the community and its contributions to the community's tax base.

EXPANDING EMPLOYMENT IN HUMAN SERVICES

The most rapidly expanding field of employment is not in industry but in services. It is in the human services, both in government and in nonprofit organizations, that jobs are multiplying fastest. As public-opinion polls show, careers in the human services are of great interest to young people. Human services, in addition to health, education, and welfare, include diverse areas. Day care centers, senior citizen centers, legal aid, retirement counseling, marriage counseling, hotlines, family planning, halfway houses, community education projects, vocational rehabilitation, self-help groups such as Alcoholics Anonymous and Weight Watchers, and human potential groups are just a few of the many services supported either by nonprofit organizations or by government agencies.[24]

The underlying activity of all human services is two-way communication on a person-to-person level, providing benefits to service workers in the form of satisfying jobs and benefits to deprived members of society, particularly the old, the poor, the handicapped, minorities, and other disadvantaged groups. Expansion of a service society will not only provide new jobs but will prove ecologically beneficial as well, since nat-

---

[23] *Ibid.*

[24] Alan Gartner and Frank Riessman, "The Service Society and Jobs," *The New York Times* (August 25, 1974).

ural resources and fossil energy are not usually involved.[25] Increased work for human services will not add to the earth's pollution and will add considerably to the quality of life in American society.

FUTURE OFFICE MANAGEMENT SYSTEMS

Every organization, whether in the production sector of the economy or in the services sector, exists in a societal environment. Society helps determine an organization's form, policy-making process, and use of available resources. The way in which an organization's management responds to daily events and proceeds toward its goals should reflect an awareness of its involvement with both the external and the internal environments. In an electronic age, organizations are best viewed not as closed but as open systems, not rigid but flexible in structure, not autocratic but democratic in philosophy, and not solely technical but also social in content.

Viewing an organization as a socio-technological system provides a basic model for future office systems. Whether a production or a services system, every organization needs a machine technology and a work pattern that harmoniously relate its human work force to its technological resources. All organization systems and subsystems, from the smallest two-person office to the largest, multinational corporate structure, are composed of elements and processes, people and relationships, equipment and procedures, management and operating policies. Certain improvements in the use of these components, made possible by modern electronic technology, have been discussed in this book: word processing, data processing, records management, telecommunications, and executive control. Knowledge of these new approaches to office systems is essential to future administrators and office workers.

Aided by a general systems approach to analysis and decision-making and by electronic technology—the most powerful human tool yet invented—management can create a future-oriented organizational structure founded on both humanistic and economic goals.

SUGGESTED READINGS

BARNOUW, ERIK. "So You Think TV Is Hot Stuff? Just You Wait," *Smithsonian*, July 1976, pp. 79–84.

CHAMPION, J.E. "Paper Piles vs. Cathode Ray Tube (CRT)," *Management World*, July 1976, pp. 21–22.

---

[25] *Ibid.*

DARROW, RICHARD W. "Employee Communications—Neglected Need," *The New York Times*, December 28, 1975, Sec. 3.

FULLER, R. BUCKMINSTER. *Operating Manual for Spaceship Earth*. New York: Simon and Schuster, 1969.

GARTNER, ALAN, and FRANK RIESSMAN. "The Service Society and Jobs," *The New York Times*, August 25, 1974.

HEILBRONER, ROBERT L. "The American Plan," *The New York Times Magazine*, January 25, 1976, pp. 9, 35–40.

JENKINS, EVAN. "Classroom Revolution: Computer Interaction," *New York Times*, June 13, 1976, Section 4, p. 9.

KLEMM, FRIEDRICH. *A History of Western Technology*. Translated by Dorothea Waley Singer. Cambridge, MA: MIT Press, 1964.

LIPPITT, GORDON L. "Transition Management—Coping: Part 1," *Management World*, January 1975, pp. 28–32.

———. "Transition Management—Coping: Part 2," *Management World*, February 1975, pp. 28–32.

"Mail Call Just Won't Be the Same," *New York Times*, May 30, 1976, Section 3.

McLUHAN, MARSHALL. *Understanding Media*. New York: McGraw-Hill Book Company, 1964.

"The Office of the Future," *Business Week*, June 30, 1975, pp. 48–84.

O'TOOLE, JAMES. "The Reserve Army of the Underemployed," *Change*, May 1975, pp. 26–33, 63.

"Selling Data to the Office of the Future," *Business Week*, June 30, 1975, p. 84.

"The Smart Machine Revolution," *Business Week*, July 5, 1976, pp. 38–44.

TOFFLER, ALVIN. *Future Shock*. New York: Bantam Books, 1971.

Appendix A

WORD PROCESSING PUBLICATIONS

Words (quarterly)

Viewpoint (monthly newsletter)

Management World (monthly)

Administrative Management (monthly)
Word Processing World (bimonthly)
Word Processing Report (twice-monthly Newsletter)

Datapro Reports on Office Systems (monthly)

Office of the Future (twice-monthly)

International Word Processing Association
Maryland Road
Willow Grove, PA 19090

Administrative Management Society
Maryland Road
Willow Grove, PA 19090

Geyer-McAllister Publications, Inc.
51 Madison Avenue
New York, NY 10010

Datapro Research Corporation
1805 Underwood Boulevard
Delran, NJ 08075

Word Processing and the American Office
37 West 72 Street
New York, NY 10023

Word Processing Publications

Word Processing (bimonthly) — Office Products Division
International Business
  Machines Corp.
Parson's Pond Drive
Franklin Lakes, NJ 07417

The Office (monthly) — Office Publications, Inc.
1200 Summer Street
Stamford, CT 06904

Modern Office Procedures (monthly) — The Industrial Publishing Co.
Division of Pittway Corporation
614 Superior Avenue, West
Cleveland, OH 44113

The Secretary (monthly) — The National Secretaries
  Association International
2440 Pershing Road
Kansas City, MO 64108

Corporate Systems (six times a year) — United Technical Publications
Division of Cox Broadcasting
  Corporation
645 Stewart Avenue
Garden City, NY 11530

Infosystems (monthly) — Hitchcock Publishing Co.
Hitchcock Building
Wheaton, IL 60187

Appendix B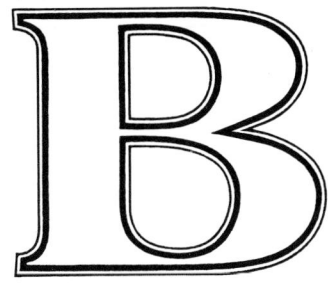

SUPPLIERS OF WORD PROCESSING EQUIPMENT

Addressograph Multigraph Corp., Varityper Division, 11 Mt. Pleasant Avenue, East Hanover, NJ 07936
Automatic Electronic Systems, Inc., 570 McCaffrey Street, Montreal, Canada H4T 1N1
Avionic Products Engineering Corp., Ford Road, Denville, NJ 07834
Base Information Systems, Inc., 437 Madison Avenue, NY, NY 10022
Comptek Research, Inc., 455 Cayuga Road, Buffalo, NY 14225
Context Corporation, 4 Ray Avenue, Burlington, MA 01803
CPT Corporation, 1001 Second Street South, Hopkins, MN 55343
Daconics Corporation, 350 Potrero Avenue, Sunnyvale, CA 94086
A. B. Dick Company, 5700 West Touhy Avenue, Chicago, IL 60648
Dictaphone Corporation, 120 Old Post Road, Rye, NY 10580
Digital Equipment Corporation, 146 Main Street, Maynard, MA 01754
Display Text Corporation, 1420 N Street, N.W., Washington, DC 20005
Editext: Word Processing, Inc., 20 Ray Avenue, Burlington, MA 01803
General Computer Systems, Inc., 16600 Dooley Road, Addison, TX 75001
Hendrix, Inc., 645 Harvey Road, Manchester, NH 03103
ICS Sales & Leasing, Inc., 313 North First, P.O. Box 281, Ann Arbor, MI 48107
International Business Machines Corporation, Office Products Division, Parson's Pond Drive, Franklin Lakes, NJ 07417
Lanier Business Products, 1700 Chantilly Drive, N.E., Atlanta, GA 30324
LCS Corporation, 31 Elm Street, Springfield, MA 01103
Lexitron Corporation, 9600 DeSoto Avenue, Chatsworth, CA 91311
Linolex/3M Company, Information Management Department, 3M Center, St. Paul, MN 55101

Micom Data Systems, Ltd., 499 St. Helene Street, Montreal, Canada H2Y 2K9
Office Communications, Inc., Veritext, 766 Palomar Avenue, Sunnyvale, CA 94086
Olivetti Corporation of America, 500 Park Avenue, New York, NY 10022
Omnitext Inc., P.O. Box 2090, 251 Jackson Plaza, Ann Arbor, MI 48106
Philips Business Systems, Inc., 175 Froehlich Farm Boulevard, Woodbury, NY 11797
Redactron/Burroughs Corporation, 100 Parkway Drive South, Hauppauge, NY 11787
Royal Typewriter Company, 150 New Park Avenue, Hartford, CT 06106
Savin Business Machines Corporation, Valhalla, NY 10595
Sony Corporation of America, 9 West 57 Street, New York, NY 10019
Sperry-Remington, Office Systems and Machines, Marietta, OH 45750
Ty-Data, Inc., 109 Northeastern Boulevard, Nashua, NH 03060
Ventek Computer Systems, Inc., 31829 West La Tienda Drive, Westlake Village, CA 91361
Vydec, Inc., 9 Vreeland Road, Florham Park, NJ 07932
Wang Laboratories, Inc., 836 North Street, Tewksbury, MA 01876
Word Processing Exchange, Inc., 3960 Varsity Drive, Ann Arbor, MI 48104
Xerox Corporation, Xerox Square, Rochester, NY 14644

Glossary of Terms

accessing The process of feeding in or extracting information or data from a computer.

administrative secretary A detail assistant who provides support services to executives in the areas of mail handling, telephones, personal files, and special projects, with little or no typing responsibility.

administrative zone An office area operated under the direction of a supervisor to provide administrative support services (including typing, dictation, filing, duplicating, mail distribution, and other errands), located in close proximity to persons who require these services. The concept provides management with flexibility to assign clerical and secretarial staff efficiently and with the ability to absorb work volume in an economical and expeditious manner.

AIOD Automatic Identification of Outward Dialing. A process that documents who is calling whom, when, and for how long.

analog computer A computer that operates with numbers represented by directly measurable quantities (as voltages, resistances, or rotations). Analog computers make approximate relational computations, such as the speedometer in an automobile.

analog transmission network The telephone lines of the Bell System designed originally to carry the fluctuating analog tones of the human voice rather than the rapid, staccato tones of the digital computer code. (See also *modem*.)

analytical machine A nineteenth-century concept by Charles Babbage in which a memory unit formed an integral part of a calculating machine, using data stored in the form of perforated cards, combined with arithmetic processes and decisions based on the machine's calculations.

AS Administrative Support.

ATS Administrative Terminal System. An IBM software package that programs computers for word processing applications.

automatic changer A device that permits the continuous central recording of dictation without the need for constantly changing the recording medium.

automatic typewriter A typewriter that captures keystrokes on magnetic media for automatic playback with minimal text editing. Also referred to as *power typewriter* and *word processing typewriter*.

Basic An easily learned computer language for the layman.

batch processing or **batching** A technique of collecting and grouping similar work for processing at one operation by a computer. Typical work method used with computers from 1958 to 1966.

binary system A system used in programming computers based on the digits 1 and 0 which combine to form numbers or, depending on the application, to signify plus and minus, on and off, yes and no.

bit A contraction of *binary digit*, the smallest unit recognized by a computer; a unit of information in the binary system corresponding to a choice between two alternatives (as 1 and 0, yes and no).

boiler plate Prerecorded model paragraphs, documents, lists, or other standard repetitive text, stored on magnetic media.

buffer A device or means used as a cushion against the shock of fluctuations between mechanical and electronic components of a system or between a driven and a driving circuit within a system.

byte A combination or sequence of adjacent bits.

cartridge A container of material (as microfilm, magnetic tape, etc.) for insertion into a larger mechanism or apparatus.

cassette A container of material, usually magnetic tape, for use in dictation equipment or other word processing machines.

central processing unit The part of a computer that consists of a core memory component, a calculations component, and an operating control component.

Centrex Central Exchange. A telephone system that permits direct dialing from outside to a specific extension phone. Unanswered calls automatically go to the switchboard for handling.

CMC IBM's Communicating Mag Card Selectric typewriter.

Cobol A highly technical computer language used by specialists.

COM Computer Output Microfilm. Microfilm that contains data produced from computer-generated signals or a recording device that converts computer data into human readable language directly on microfilm.

COM recorder A device that produces computer printouts of documents or data on microfilm. An on-line recorder is wired directly to the computer; an off-line recorder with a tape drive operates independently by processing magnetic tape from a computer.

communication transmission modes Manner or style of sending communications, as conversational, Telex (7 characters per second), TWX (10 cps), IBM CMC (15 cps), Xerox CMC (120 cps), or computer high speed batch.

communicating word processor Various makes of communicating typewriters.

computer A machine for performing calculations. An electronic computer performs calculations automatically.

computer console The main terminal through which the computer operator enters program instructions and monitors the machine by use of an electronic keyboard.

computer terminal A typewriter wired to a computer for use as an input/output device.

Glossary of Terms 167

continuous loop See *endless loop* recorders.
correspondence management A word processing system.
CPS Certified Professional Secretary; (lower case) characters per second.
CPU Central Processing Unit of a computer.
CRT Cathode Ray Tube used in video-display terminals of electronic word processing systems.
data Factual material, especially that used as a basis for discussion or decision.
DE Dictation Equipment.
dedicated slave A unit kept exclusively for one kind of work under the control of a master unit.
Diablo Trade name of a high-speed printer used in computer word processing.
digital computer A computer that operates with numbers expressed directly as digits in a decimal, binary, or other system, for example, an odometer in an automobile.
digital transmission network A network designed to carry directly the rapid, rat-a-tat signals of the digital computer code, unlike the Bell System telephone lines. See also *modem*.
discrete media Individual magnetic belts, tapes, or disks that can be removed from a dictation machine.
disk A form of magnetic recording media used to store data or information. See also *floppy disk*.
disk storage See *random access*.
distributed processing A decentralized approach to office systems focusing on a manager and a department (rather than a monolithic system for an entire division or company) and using a communications network of minicomputers to perform the work of a large central computer.
DP Data Processing or operations for converting (as by computers) crude information into usable or storable form.
duplexing A process that permits both sides of a single page to be copied on a photocopy machine.
EDP Electronic Data Processing.
electromechanical Of or relating to electrically powered machines or tools.
electronic computer An electronic machine that automatically performs complex calculations.
electronic keyboard A typewriter keyboard that operates electronically and, therefore, silently.
electronic mail Communications transmitted in digital code between distant locations and reproduced in paper format at the destination by means of computers, communicating word processors, facsimile, Telex/TWX, or Mailgram.
endless loop recorders A continuous flow dictation system in which magnetic tape is sealed in a tank and loops around constantly; dictation on the tape can be played back a short distance from where the person is dictating.
ENIAC Electronic Numerical Integrator and Calculator; the first machine to use electronic tubes in calculating, developed by John W. Mauchly and J. Presper Eckert (1942-1946).
facsimile A scanning device that transmits over telephone lines printed material or photographs, one page at a time, for reproduction at the point of destination.

floppy disk A form of magnetic recording media that permits random access to stored data, as compared with a rigid disk used also in computer memories.

flowchart A form or diagram that indicates the various steps or processes required to complete a job or project.

Fortran A special language used for programming computers.

hard copy A typed or printed document on paper.

hardware The devices and machines that make up the components of a computer, as compared with *software* (programs used to control a computer's operations).

input The process of feeding information into a computer.

input/output Also referred to as I/O. A broad term that refers to a terminal used for communicating with a computer, to the information processed while communicating, and to the process of communicating itself.

integrated circuit A tiny complex of electronic components and their connections produced in or on a small slice of silicon. Based on solid logic technology as compared with hard-wired or electromechanical relay logic systems.

interconnect device A device required by AT&T as protection on a customer's premises between the Bell System's telephone lines and privately-owned telephone equipment.

interface The point at which the Bell System equipment is connected to privately-owned telephone equipment; the place at which independent systems meet and communicate with each other.

IWP International Word Processing Association.

key system A group of multibutton telephone instruments that provide access to all central office trunk lines as well as intercommunication connections for everyone in an organization.

keyboard An assemblage of systematically arranged keys by which a machine is operated.

keypunch A machine with a typewriter-like keyboard used to prepare data for the computer by punching cards with preassigned codes. Codes are transferred to cards by keypunch operators.

labor-intensive With labor rather than machines a major factor in office work. The workers' salaries represent a major part of the total cost of operating an office.

log sheet A record kept in a word processing center to keep track of incoming and outgoing work.

logging The process of entering incoming work on a log sheet in order to control work flow.

LSI Large-Scale Integration or monolithic circuitry. See also *MST*.

magnetic recording The process of recording sound, data, or a television program by producing varying local magnetization of a moving tape, wire, or disk.

magnetic tape A ribbon of thin paper or plastic, coated for use in magnetic recording.

MC/ST or **Mag Card** Magnetic Card Selectric Typewriter.

medium (*pl.* **media**) A means of effecting or conveying something; e.g., tape, disks, paper, or microfilm are media used to convey words or data.

memory typewriter A typewriter that stores keyboarded material and plays it back automatically.

message switching A store-and-forward process used in Western Union's Mailgram service by which each Mailgram message received in one day is stored in a central computer then transmitted at night to a post office teleprinter located nearest to the Mailgram's addressee.

MICR Magnetic Ink Character Readers. See OCR.

microcomputer A tiny computer consisting of a microprocessor or CPU on a chip of silicon and two memory chips, one for moving data in and out of the CPU, and one to program the CPU.

microfiche A form of microfilm that represents usually a single 8½ x 11-inch page. Up to 98 microfiche can be mounted on a single index-size aperture card.

microfilm A medium for recording permanent documents reduced in size so that optical magnifying devices are required for reading.

microprocessor A microscopic logic circuit on a chip of silicon that performs over one million calculations a second. It is based on MST, an outgrowth of solid logic technology that first produced the integrated circuit.

microwave A very short electromagnetic wave.

minicomputer A small computer, fast in computation, but with limited input/output and secondary storage.

MIS Management Information System.

mode A particular form or variety of something; a form or manner of expression; a manner of doing something; the vibration pattern of electromagnetic waves.

modem A device that modulates the rapid, rat-a-tat digital signals of the computer code before transmitting them over telephone lines, a network originally designed for the slower, fluctuating, analog tones of the human voice. The signals are demodulated to digital again at the point of destination.

MST Monolithic Systems Technology used in microprocessors, a byproduct of the space program technology.

MT/SC Magnetic Tape Selectric Composer.

MT/ST Magnetic Tape Selectric Typewriter. An IBM electric typewriter with a memory capability that simultaneously records typed material on paper and on a magnetic tape mounted on a changeable cartridge and wired to the typewriter.

multiplexing A process of scanning and splitting a single conversation pathway into different segments in the time division mode of PBX operation. Each conversation has its own time slot, thus eliminating electro-mechanical switching.

OCR Optical Character Recognition or optical scanner. A scanning device and magnetic ink character reader that permits direct input to and processing by the computer of bank checks, airline tickets, and typed documents, without human intervention.

off-line Relating to a peripheral computer device that operates independently of the CPU.

on-line Relating to a direct connection wired to the CPU of a computer.

PABX Private Automatic Branch Exchange.

PBX Private Branch Exchange.

peripheral equipment Any equipment in data processing and word processing that works in conjunction with the CPU of the computer but is not an integral part, such as input terminals, printers, keypunch, tape drive, OCR.

photocomposition A form of composing text for reproduction by means of characters photographed on film.

playback, playout The process of automatically typing out recorded text on a word processor or the process of listening to recorded dictation on dictation equipment.

power typewriter An automatic electronic typewriter that can play back recorded text by itself at up to 350 words a minute.

prerecorded Recorded in advance for use in repetitive typing, such as paragraphs recorded on magnetic media for use in form letters.

principal An executive or an individual in an organization who originates paperwork and needs secretarial support.

printer A device used for printing; a machine attached to a computer for the production of printed documents or data from material stored in the computer's memory.

private wire system A system for recording dictation that is not connected to telephone company lines.

program A set of instructions to control the operations of automated machines such as computers and word processing systems.

pulse code amplitude A technical term for a type of signal modulation considered more economical by AT&T as the basic operational process for its new electronic PABX.

pulse code modulation A technical term for a type of signal modulation, which is a basic operational process used in electronic PABXs; essentially a digital technique. See also *modem*.

Qume A brand of printer, used with computer word processing systems, that prints out text at 525 words a minute.

random access A disk storage technique in word processing and data processing that permits access to individual transactions randomly in a fraction of a second as compared with the serial nature of tape storage, thus potentially increasing the speed of output units.

reader A device for projecting a readable image of a microfilm image.

record To cause vocal sounds or keystrokes to be registered as on magnetic tape, card, or disk, in reproducible form.

recorder A unit in a dictation system that records the dictation on magnetic media.

recording media A variety of magnetic devices used for the recording of dictation, such as magnetic belts, magnetic disks, and magnetic tapes enclosed in cassettes or cartridges, providing anywhere from six minutes to ninety minutes of recording time.

remote access The capability of making use of from a distance.

scanning To bring under a moving electron beam for conversion of light and dark picture or image values into corresponding electrical values to be transmitted by facsimile or television.

secretary One employed traditionally to handle correspondence and manage routine clerical and detail work for an office executive; one entrusted with the secrets or confidences of a superior.

secretary, administrative One responsible for providing administrative support to more than one executive or principal in such matters as opening and distributing mail, answering telephones and taking messages, keeping private correspondence files and records, conducting special projects involving research, and drafting reports or letters for the principals.

secretary, correspondence or **word processing** A typing specialist responsible for transcribing from dictation equipment or handwritten drafts; a machine-oriented person who understands the logic of automated typing equipment and how to use its capabilities to best advantage in the production of typed documents.

selectric An electric typewriter introduced by IBM in the early 1960s and featuring a moving ball type element.

serial storage The storage of data in a set sequence, as on a magnetic tape, which usually means a longer search time when retrieving as compared with random access to data stored on floppy disks.

shared logic system A word processing system in which operators at a number of keyboard terminals use the memory and processing powers of one computer's CPU simultaneously.

single element A term that describes a typing mechanism, such as the IBM Selectric's ball or the Xerox printwheel, which contains all the type characters on a single unit.

slave typewriter See *dedicated slave*.

software The program or set of instructions that control a computer's operations. See also *hardware*.

solid logic technology See *integrated circuit*.

space division An electromechanical PABX mode of operation, used with dial telephones, that requires large areas of space for switching relay mechanisms. This equipment is used in making step-by-step connections between two distant users. Each turn of the dial activates a switching relay point to physically set up a talking path or network to the party being called. When the caller hangs up, the network becomes deactivated and ready for the next call. This mode of operation is used by most PABX systems.

split keyboarding Keyboarding and editing material on one word processing unit and playing it out on another.

stand-alone A term applied to machines that operate independently and are not connected to other machines.

station A work place to which an individual is assigned in a word processing center; a telephone extension or a teletypewriter terminal in telecommunications.

store and forward A technique used in electronic mail whereby a number of messages are collected and held in a computer for high-speed transmission in a single operation. See also *message switching*.

switch coding or **switching** A process of controlling incoming and outgoing calls to and from a number of telephones; a process of merging information from two magnetic cards or tapes to produce a single document automatically on a word processing machine.

switched digital service A service that provides almost instantaneous connection between one computer terminal and another located anywhere along a network for the transmission of digital data. On a switched network, all calls go to a central computerized switch that directs them and completes the connection in less than one second.

systems approach A way of viewing a situation or an assemblage of interrelated items as an organized whole, rather than a number of separate entities considered individually. In word processing, a systems approach to the production of typed documents considers each component in the system—office workers, procedures, and equipment—not as separate entities but rather in relationship to the whole organization of the office. The goal of a systems approach is the performance of work tasks by everyone concerned in the most efficient manner, at the least cost, and in the fastest time possible.

tank recorder See *endless loop recorder.*

telecommunications A science that deals with the study of communication at a distance, as by cable, radio, telegraphy, telephone, or television.

teleprinter or **TELEX** A machine operated by a teletypist who phones another teletypist at a distant location; once the connection is made, the two teletypists communicate by typing back and forth while the machines record their messages in writing. A service offered by Western Union, the TWX/Telex network takes in some 225,000 installations at major business locations across the United States, Canada, and Mexico.

teletypewriter or **TWX** See *teleprinter.*

terminal A device attached to the end of a wire or cable or to an electrical apparatus such as a computer for sending and receiving information; an input/output device; a communicating typewriter.

text The main body of printed or written matter on a page.

text editing The practice of recording and revising information, using electronic typing systems.

text editor An electronic typing system that records typed material on magnetic media and permits revisions and corrections by backspacing and typing over information to be changed.

text processor An automatic or electronic typewriter.

textverarbeitung The term for "word processing" first used in Germany in 1965 by IBM.

thought tank Endless loop dictation machine made by Dictaphone.

time division A PABX mode of operation, used with pushbutton telephones, that eliminates the need for physical switching mechanisms because the tones keyed in by the caller open a general talking pathway to the party being called. See also *space division.*

time division multiplexing The process of splitting a general talking pathway in a telephone system into different segments of time by means of a scanning operation so that several messages or conversations are transmitted simultaneously, each in its own time slot, along the same general pathway.

time sharing A commercial service in which clients purchase limited segments of a multiprogramming, multiprocessing, and multiple-access computer as well as computer-related services. A typewriter terminal in the client's office is connected to the out-of-house computer through normal telephone lines, and the system operates on a "pay as you use it" basis.

touch-tone AT&T's push-button telephone instrument.

transcriber or **transcribing unit** A machine component of a dictation system used to play back recorded dictation to a transcriptionist.

transcriptionist A person who transcribes by typing out recorded dictation into document form.

transistor An electronic device that replaced electronic tubes in computers,

Glossary of Terms

resulting in significant reductions in physical size of computer systems and in vastly superior logic and core memories.

trunk A hookup between two telephone exchanges for making connections between subscribers.

turnkey software A computer program that provides the operator with complete step-by-step instructions for using the system.

typing pool A centralized office area set aside for production typing where work is assigned to the typing staff under the close control of a typing supervisor.

UNIVAC Universal Automatic Computer, the first commercial electronic computer, installed in the Census Bureau in 1951 and at General Electric in Louisville, Kentucky, in 1954.

video-display terminal A device similar to a television screen used to display information or data electronically when attached to a computer or to a word processing system.

VOR Voice Operated Relay. A device that activates the recorder unit of a dictation machine when voice sounds come in over a telephone line and automatically stops the recorder after five seconds of silence to eliminate the recording of silence.

word processing center A centralized office area set aside for the production of typed documents by technicians operating automatic word processing equipment.

word processing system A planned interrelation of personnel, procedures, and equipment within an office environment or work specialization and controls to facilitate the production of typed documents in a cost-effective manner.

word processor Another term for word processing typewriter or text processor.

work-group approach A system employed by a group of company executives with their own word processing center for heavy typing tasks and with administrative secretaries to handle light typing and other assignments. Both word processing and administrative secretaries also operate computer terminals in this approach.

WP Word Processing. The transformation of ideas and information into a readable form of communication through the efficient organization of people, procedures, and equipment; the automation of document production.

WP/AS Word Processing/Administrative Support

wpm words per minute

Xerox print wheel A unique, electronically-driven type of element containing one type character on each spoke of a wheel, used in the Xerox 800 typing system.

Index

Accessing, 108
Administrative Management
  Association, 45
Administrative Management Society, 37
Administrative secretary, 4, 40–43
  characteristics of, 50–51
  function of, 32–34, 41
  human aspects of:
    career paths, 67–68
    negative, 65–66
    positive, 66–67
  qualifications required, 54
  senior, 54
  skills required, 7, 50–51
  in team concept, 41–42
  training programs for, 68
  as word originator, 32–33, 42
Administrative support, position
  descriptions, 54–56
Administrative support center, 41–43,
  54–55
Administrative zone, 43–46
Aiken, Howard, 103
AIOD (automatic identification of outward
  dialing), 130
Air Canada, 74–75
American Hospital Supply Corporation,
  122–23
American Telephone & Telegraph
  Company (AT&T), 121–23, 127, 130
Analog computer, 102, 121
Analytical machine, 102
ATS (Administrative Terminal System), 154
Automatic Sequence Controlled
  Calculator, 103
Automatic typewriters, 11–17, 151

Automation, 60–62
  challenge of, 76–77
  rationalization of work and, 62–63

Babbage, Charles, 102–03
Batch processing, 105
Bell & Howell Company, 133
Bell System, 121–22, 127, 128, 130
Bergman & Barth, 96–98
Binary system, 103
Boole, George, 103
Burroughs Corporation, 106
Business letter, cost of, 7–8

Case studies, 9, 79–100
CBX (Computerized Branch Exchange), 130
Centralized dictation equipment, 44
  discrete media, 23–26
  endless loop, 26–28
Certified Professional Secretary (CPS), 36
Chevron Oil Company Geophysical
  Division, 92–93
CH2M Hill, 90–92
Clerical work:
  changing positions in, 7–8
  cost of, 8
  See also Secretarial work
Clerk/messenger, 54
COM (computer output microfilm), 137–40
Communicating Mag Card Selectric
  Typewriter (CMC), 17–18, 91, 108–09
Communicating typewriters, 17–18,
  108–09, 91, 125–26
Communications, 119–21
  management-employee, 157–58
  See also Telecommunications

Communicator computers, 106
Comptek Accutext, 115
Computer console, 101
Computer terminal, 100
Computerized office switchboards, 128, 144, 152
Computers, 2, 9, 10, 21, 32, 101–16
  communicating typewriters connected to, 108–09
  electronic, development of, 103–04
  first generation, 104
  future systems, 151–56
  historical development of, 102–03
  microcomputers, 18–21, 93, 95, 96, 99, 110, 116
    second computer revolution and, 115–16
    word processing systems, 18–21, 116
  minicomputers:
    use of, 107–08
    word processing systems, 110–15
  office workers and, 149–51
  portable, 152
  second generation, 104–06
  third generation, 106–07
  time sharing, 109–10
  See also Management information systems (MIS)
Compu-TEXT, 96–97, 112, 113
Congressional Research Service (CRS), 20
Copier machines, 140–41, 151–52
Correspondence management, *see* Records management
Correspondence secretary, 3, 7, 52
  See also Word processing secretary
Correspondence specialist/technical advisor, 53
CPT Corporation, 15
CPU (central processing unit), 109, 110, 115
Crown Center Hotel, Kansas City, Missouri, 80–81
CRT microcomputer systems, 18–21, 93, 95, 96, 99, 110, 116

Dacom, Inc., 124
Dartnell Corporation, 7–8, 38
Data processing:
  division of labor and, 63–64
  electronic, 2, 9, 10, 32, 64
Data transmission networks, 121–24, 152
Datapax PBX, 129
Dataphone Digital Service, 122
Datasystem 310W, 111–12

Data-Text, 113
Datran (Data Transmission Company), 122–24
Del Monte Corporation, 85–87
Dennison Manufacturing Company, 140
Dick, A. B., Company, Inc., 140
Dictaphone secretary, 3
Dictaphone Thought Tank System 193, 26, 27, 83
Dictation:
  case studies, 81, 84, 86, 90
  traditional methods of, 38–39
Dictation equipment, 22–28
  centralized, 44
    discrete media, 23–26
    endless loop, 26–28
  efficiency, 8
  importance of, 22–23
  telephone systems used with, 28–30
  training executives in use of, 40
Digital computer, 102–121
Digital Equipment Corporation, 107, 111–12
Dimension PBX, 127, 130
Discrete media dictation machines, 23–26
Disk storage, 105
Distributed processing approach, 153
Division of labor:
  data processing and, 63–64
  word processing and, 65

Eastman Kodak Company, 133, 140
Eckert, J. Presper, 103–04
Economic planning, 156–57
Eldorado 14, 115
Electronic data processing (EDP), 2, 9, 10, 32, 64
Electronic mail, 125-26, 152
Electronic technology, future effects of, 147–59
  on equipment, 151–53
  expanding employment in human services and, 158–59
  management-employee communication and, 157–58
  on management systems, 159
  on organizational structures, 156–57
  on procedures, 153–56
  on workers, 148–51
Electronic keyboard, 101
Employee morale, 70–74
Employee Retirement Income Security Act of 1974, 157-58
Endless loop dictation equipment, 26–28

Index

ENIAC (Electronic Numerical Integrator and Calculator), 103–04, 114, 115
Equal opportunity, 59
Equipment, see Word processing equipment
Executive assistant, 44
Executive control, 119, 142–45
Executive Mag Card Typewriter, 80, 91

Facsimile, 121, 124
Federal Communications Commission (FCC), 122, 123, 127, 128, 130
Floppy disk, 110
Ford, Henry, 63

General Computer Systems, 113
Goldschmidt, F., 150
Grace, W. R., & Company, 87–88

Hardware, computer, 111
Hewlett-Packard, 107
Hoff, M. E., Jr., 115
Hollerith, Herman, 103
Honeywell, Inc., 106
Houston Lighting & Power Company, 98–100
Human services, expanding employment in, 158–59

IBM Corporation, 5, 7, 11, 13, 68, 103, 107
  communicating Mag Card Selectric Typewriter (CMC), 17–18, 91, 108
  Executive Mag Card Typewriter, 80, 91
  5100 Portable Computer, 152
  future office systems, 153–54
  Mag Card/A Typewriter, 13, 15
  Mag Card II Typewriter, 4, 13, 14, 82, 85, 89, 90, 91
  Magnetic Card Selectric Typewriter (MC/ST), 5, 13, 85
  Magnetic Tape Selectric Typewriter (MT/ST), 5, 12–13, 86, 88, 89
  Selectric, 11, 12, 13
  Series III Copier/Duplicator, 141
  6:5 Cartridge System, 24–25, 82
  System/360 Computer, 106, 109
Illinois Department of Revenue, 138–40
Illinois National Bank of Springfield, 82–83
Incentives, 75
Industrial goods-producing era, 60, 61
Intel Corporation 8080 Minicomputer, 116
Internal Revenue Service, 125
International Business Machines Corporation, see IBM Corporation

Job satisfaction, 71–73
Job specialization, 32
Job titles, new, 2–5, 56
Junior correspondence secretary, 52

Key system, 130
Kimberly-Clark Corporation, 68

Labor, division of, see Division of labor
Labor Statistics, Bureau of, 9, 34, 38, 60, 61
Lanier Business Products:
  Nyematic VIP System, 26
  Tel-Edisette System, 23–24
LCS Corporation Compu-TEXT, 96–97, 112, 113
Lexitron Corporation Videotype Text Professor, 20
Library of Congress, Congressional Research Service of, 94–96
Linolex Systems, Inc., see 3M Company
Little, Reg, 74

Mag card secretary, 3
Mag Card/A Typewriter, 13, 15
Mag Card II Typewriter, 3, 13, 14, 82, 85, 89, 90, 91
Magnetic Card Selectric Typewriter (MC/ST), 5, 13, 85
Magnetic ink character readers, 106
Magnetic Tape Selectric Typewriter (MT/ST), 5, 12–13, 86, 88, 89
Mail electronic, 125–26, 152
Mailgrams, 126, 152
Management information system (MIS), 9, 10, 119–45
  executive control, 119, 142–45
  records management, 133–42
    defined, 133
    microfilm, 133, 134–40
    photocopiers, 140–41
    phototypesetting, 141–42
  telecommunications, 121–31
    data transmission networks, 121–24
    defined, 121
    electronic mail, 125–26, 152
    facsimile, 121, 124–25
    future, 152–53
    mailgrams, 126, 152
    office telephone switchboards, 127–31, 144, 152
    telephone technology, 129–31, 133
    TWX and Telex, 109, 126–27
Manager, word processing/administrative support system, 55–56

Mark I, 103
Mauchly, John W., 103–04
MC/ST, see Magnetic Card Selectric Typewriter
Mechanization of office work, 69–70
Message switching, 126
Micro 4000 System, 139
Microcomputers, 18–21, 93, 95, 96, 99, 110, 116
 second computer revolution and, 115–16
 word processing systems, 18–21, 116
Microfiche, 134
Microfilm, 133, 134–40
Microfilm duplicator, 136
Microprocessor, 18
Microwave Communications, Inc., 122
Mills, C. Wright, 69–70
Minicomputers:
 use of, 107–108
 word processing systems, 110–15
MIS, see Management information systems (MIS)
Modem (modulator-demodulator), 121
Monolithic systems technology (MST), 115
Morale, 70–74
Motivation, 74–75
Mountainside Hospital, Montclair, New Jersey, 84–85
MT/ST, see Magnetic Tape Selectric Typewriter (MT/ST)

National Broadcasting Company, 67
National Secretaries Association, 36, 37–38
Navy Recruiting Command, 125–26
NCR Corporation, 106
Northwest Region Zellerbach Paper Company, 136–37
Nyematic VIP System, 26

Office costs:
 in relation to total cost, 7, 32
 underutilization of secretaries and, 37–38
office equipment, future, 151–53
Office management systems, future, 159
Office procedures, future, 153–56
Office work:
 mechanization of, 69–70
 in word processing secretarial mode, 39
Office workers, future, 148–51
Olivetti S-14 "Mastermind," 15
Optical character recognition (OCR), 113
Optical scanners, 106

Organizational structures:
 computer technology and, 142–45
 future, 156–57
Originating, defined, 120

PABX (private automatic branch exchange), 127, 144, 154
Paperwork, decline in, 147–48
PBX (private branch exchange), 28–30, 127–31
People-oriented word processing, 74–76
PepsiCo International, 67–68
Philips/Norelco 260 Automatic Dictation System, 24, 25
Photocopiers, 140–41
Phototypesetting, 141–42
Pitney Bowes, 140
Portable computer, 152
Private automatic branch exchange (PABX), 127, 144, 154
Private branch exchange (PBX) systems, 28–30, 126–31
Production, defined, 120
Productivity, 37–39
 case studies, 81, 83, 84, 85, 86, 88, 90, 92, 93, 97–98, 100
 executive, 38
Professional secretary, 67
Programming techniques, 105
Progressional secretary, 67
Proofreader/process control coordinator, 53
Pulse code modulation, 130

Quantum Science Corporation, 144
Quindata Company, 15

Random access file, 135
Rapifax Corporation, 125
Recordak Prostar film processor, 136–37
Records management, 133–42
 defined, 133
 microfilm, 133, 134–40
 photocopiers, 140–41
 phototypesetting, 141–42
Redactron Corporation, 5, 15
 automatic typewriters, 9, 98
 Redactor Communicating Typewriter, 18
 text editing typewriters, 83
Remington No. 1 typewriter, 6, 103
Remington Rand Office Machines, 104, 140
Remote access, 134
Riland, Lane, 75
Roll film, 134

Index

Rolm Corporation, 130
Royal Typewriter Company, 140

Satellite networks, 122
Savin Business Machines, 15
Secretarial utilization, 37–38, 40–41
Secretarial work:
  historical development of, 6
  nature of, 36–37
  salaries, 7–8
  traditional, 7, 33
  traditional positions in, 34–36
  underutilization and, 37–38
  in word processing:
    changing positions and, 7–8
    nontyping duties, see Administrative secretary
    typing duties, see Word processing secretary
  work habits, 40
Secretary:
  defined, 36
  functions of, 35–36
  See also Administrative secretary; Secretarial work; Word processing secretary
Selectric typewriter, 11, 12, 13
  Communicating Mag Card, 17–18, 91, 108–09
  Executive Mag Card, 80, 81
  Mag Card/A, 13, 15
  Mag Card II, 5, 13, 14, 82, 85, 89, 90, 91
  Magnetic Card (MC/ST), 5, 13, 85
  Magnetic Tape (MT/ST), 5, 12–13, 86, 88, 89
Senior administrative secretary, 54
Serial storage, 110
Shorthand, historical development of, 6
Software, computer, 105, 111
Sony Remote Dictation System, 25–26
Sperry Rand Corporation, 5, 15, 106
Stand-alone units, 20
Standard Oil of Indiana, 67
Stanford Research Institute, 7, 8
State National Bank of Connecticut, 83–84
Stenographers, 6, 34–35
Stewart-Warner Corporation, 125
Store and forward, 126
Supervisor:
  administrative support center, 54–55
  word processing, 53–54
  word processing/administrative support center, 55
Supervisory controls, 32

Switchboards, 127–31, 144, 152
Switching system, 122
Systems approach, see Word processing systems

Taylor, Frederick W., 63
Teachers Insurance and Annuity Association and College Retirement Equities Fund, 88–90
Tel-Edisette System, 23–24
Telecommunications, 121–31
  data transmission networks, 121–24, 152
  defined, 121
  electronic mail, 125–26, 152
  facsimile, 121, 124–25
  future, 152–53
  mailgrams, 126, 152
  office telephone switchboards, 127–31, 144, 152
  telephone technology, 129–31, 133
  TWX and Telex, 109, 126–27
Telephone switchboards, 127–31, 144, 152
Telephone technology, 129–31, 133
Teleprinters, 121, 126–27
Telex, 109, 126–27
Thought Tank System 193, 26, 27, 83
3M Company
  facsimile, 124–25
  Linolex 4000 Word Processor, 115
  Linolex Video Text Editor, 20, 21
  microfilm, 133
Time division multiplexing, 129
Time share computing, 109–10
Training, 68, 74–75
Trans World Airlines, Inc., 142
Trendata Corporation, 15
Turnkey software, 112–13
TWX, 18, 126–27
Ty-Data, Inc., 5, 15
Typewriters, 11–18, 151
  communicating, 17–18, 91, 108–09, 125–26
  See also Selectric typewriters
Typing pools, 39
Typists:
  functions of, 34
  See also Word processing secretary

UNIVAC (Universal Automatic Computer), 104
Utilization, defined, 120

Video-display systems, 18–21
Video telephone, 153

Voice operated relay (VOR), 24
Vydec, Inc., 5, 20

Wang Laboratories, 5, 15, 107
   1220 TC, 18
   System 1200 Cassette Typewriter, 19
   text editing typewriters, 83
Western Union Telegraph Company, 126
White-collar jobs, 9–10
Women:
   equal opportunity for, 59
   new career opportunities for, 9
Word originators, 32–33, 42
Word processing, 1–10
   case studies, 9, 79–100
   computer, *See* Computers
   cost reduction and, 8
   defined, 2, 32
   equipment, *see* Word processing equipment
   goal of, 2
   human element in, 9–10
   job titles, 2–5, 56
   management information systems and, *see* Management information systems (MIS)
   publications, 161–62
   qualifications required, 52–54
   systems, *see* Word processing systems
Word processing administrator, 3
Word processing center, 45–46, 77
   employee morale in, 70–74
   supervisor, 55
Word processing cycle, 120–21
Word processing equipment, 7, 32, 77
   automatic typewriters, 11–17, 151
   communicating typewriters, 17–18, 91, 108–09, 125–26
   computer-based, *see* Computers
   cost reduction and, 8
   dictation equipment, 22–28
      discrete media, 23–26
      efficiency, 8
      endless loop, 26–28
      importance of, 22–23
      telephone systems used with, 28–30
   suppliers of, 163–64
Word processing secretary, 4, 32–33
   characteristics of, 49–50
   function of, 32, 33
   human aspects of, 65, 68–69, 77
      negative, 68–69
      standards, 69

morale of, 70–74
   position descriptions, 52–54
   skills required, 7, 49–50
Word processing specialist/librarian, 53
Word processing supervisor, 33
Word processing systems, 1, 31–46
   administrative support function in, *see* Administrative secretary
   administrative zone, 43–45
   automation, 60–62
      challenge of, 76–77
      rationalization of work and, 62–63
   costs:
      secretarial utilization and, 37–38
      in word processing secretarial mode, 39
   defined, 2, 32–34
   dictation, traditional methods of, 38–39
   division of labor:
      data processing and, 63–64
      word processing and, 65
   flexibility of, 45–46
   functional areas of, 120
   goal of, 31
   productivity and, 37–39
   secretarial positions, traditional, 34–36
   secretarial work, nature of, 36–37
   systems approach to office paperwork, 31–32
   transcription, traditional methods of, 39
   work habits affected by, 40
   See also Word processing equipment
Word processing technology, human aspects of, 59–77
   administrative secretary, 66–68
      career paths for, 67–68
      negative aspects of job, 65–66
      positive aspects of job, 66–67
   employee morale, 70–74
   mechanization of office work, 69–70
   people-oriented word processing, 74–76
   word processing secretary, 65, 77
      negative aspects of job, 68–69
      standards, 69
Work-group approach, 154

Xerox Corporation, 16, 68
   800 Electronic Typing System, 5, 16, 17, 18, 87
   future office systems, 153–55
   photocopiers, 140
   Telecopier, 124–25

Yankee Group, 125